South of Seattle

Notes on Life in the Northwest Woods

South of Seattle

Notes on Life in the Northwest Woods

James LeMonds

Foreword by
Robert Michael Pyle

1997
Mountain Press Publishing Company
Missoula, Montana

Cover art (*Better Days Ahead*) and interior illustrations
copyright © 1997 John Ely

Many of the essays in this book first appeared in magazines and newspapers:
"Northwest Dreaming" in *The Oregonian*, March 1994 and *Seattle Weekly*,
May 1994; "Voices from the Old World" in *Timberline Magazine*, Spring 1994;
"The Glossy Prints" in the *Sunriver Sun*, Winter 1994; "The Felling Fields"
in *Seattle Weekly*, January 1994 and *Life in Toutle Country*, Spring 1995; "Risen
from the Ashes" (in a different form) in *The Tacoma News-Tribune*, May 1995;
and "Scripture for the Land" in *Bear Essential*, Winter 1995. We gratefully
acknowledge their editors and staffs.

PRINTED IN THE UNITED STATES OF AMERICA
PRINTED ON RECYCLED PAPER

Library of Congress Cataloging-in-Publication Data

LeMonds, James, 1950–
    South of Seattle : notes on life in the Northwest woods / James
Lemonds.
        p.   cm.
    ISBN 0-87842-363-X (alk. paper)
    1. Castle Rock (Wash.)—Social life and customs—Anecdotes.
2. Country life—Washington (State)—Castle Rock—Anecdotes.
3. Castle Rock (Wash.)—Biography—Anecdotes. 4. Lemonds,
James, 1950–   —Anecdotes. I. Title.
F899.C38L46   1997
979.7'88—dc21   97-28352
                                                                       CIP

Mountain Press Publishing Company
P.O. Box 2399 • Missoula, MT 59806
(406) 728-1900

For Sherry,

who always makes everything right

PRAISE FOR

South of Seattle

❧ "James LeMonds brings us unexpected treasure, like a glimpse of gold in a mountain stream, in his loving description of life in Castle Rock, Washington. . . . LeMonds examines the big issues of the Pacific Northwest—the preservation of the last old-growth forests, the conflicts with wildlife, and impending loss of lifestyle—with wisdom and a humane vision that never fails."

—Mary Clearman Blew, author of *All But the Waltz*

❧ "His quirky yet universal themes are the ones that the second-comers everywhere have faced: getting along with other species, letting go of the ancestors without losing the stories, learning how to behave on the fringes of the old frontier, and remembering and preserving what is good. James LeMonds catches the fire and buzz of life in his yet-rural, part-wild corner of the West as well and as incisively as any writer I know."

—Robert Michael Pyle, author of *Wintergreen*

❧ "To write with affection about the people and the place you love is one of the most dangerous things for a modern American author to attempt. Luckily, LeMonds has the knowledge and skill to pull it off."

—Robert Leo Heilman, author of
Overstory: Zero, Real Life in Timber Country

❧ "South of Seattle is a clearly written, carefully observed, often poignant meditation on life and land in the Pacific Northwest. Often personal and always attentive to detail, LeMonds' book adds a thoughtful and generous voice to the vigorous conversation over the fate and future of the modern Far Corner."

—Brian Doyle, Editor of *Portland Magazine*

❧ "South of Seattle is a worthy addition to the testament of place. LeMonds . . . chronicles the nature of the land and the routes we take to arrive at ourselves."

—Douglas Spangle,
Associate Editor of *Rain City Review*

❧ "Jim LeMonds has lived in the misty forests that surround the Cowlitz River all his life, and his personal essays are firmly rooted to the place."

—Jack Nisbet, author of
Sources of the River and *Purple Flat Top*

Contents

Acknowledgments

Thanks to Mom and Dad for the stories; to Kim and Kami for their love and support; to John for the art; and to Larry for helping me get started.

Thanks also to Douglas Spangle and Brian Doyle, who read the manuscript and provided direction, and to Kathleen Ort at Mountain Press Publishing for her patience and expertise.

I am especially indebted to Bob and Thea for making me believe it was possible.

Foreword

"WE KNOW SO LITTLE ABOUT THE WORLD WE INHABIT," writes Jim LeMonds in one of the essays that follows. How mournfully true a statement this is. Unlike every other organism, from banana slugs to Bigfoot, we thrive in epic ignorance of our surroundings—how they work, who lives there, what they do, and how (above all) to share the provident allocations of the land. But that is a corporate "we." In truth, Jim LeMonds is not one of those who knows so little of the world he inhabits. As all the essays in *South of Seattle* show, he knows his home ground with an intimacy "we" all might aim for and admire.

Jim is my neighbor, in watershed terms. He and Sherry live across the rounded, ragged tops of the Willapa Hills from where Thea and I have gone to ground on Gray's River. His creeks flow into the Cowlitz River, which empties into the Columbia a little above where Gray's River debouches into the Great River of the West. So while it might take ninety minutes to drive between our homes on pavement, or five hours on logging roads, the rain that collects in Growler's Gulch eventually mixes with the moisture that continually bathes our bit of Willapa and collects in its little creek. What we share besides the rain is these subtle hills, and our devotion to dwelling among them as best we can. What I can never know as Jim knows is the sense of in-dwelling, of home-staying: born, raised, and fledged in one place, gone away briefly and returned, finally lodged for the long haul in his own natal ground.

Seattle and its precincts so dominate most people's idea of western Washington that the notion of anything worthy of literature lying between Puget Sound and Portland might come as a shock, or at least a dull surprise. But read these pieces and prepare to change your mind. A slew of often shrunken, sometimes stable little towns and hamlets adorn the Maritime Northwest like lilies (or beer cans) strewn across a great green pond. Every one—Elma, Adna, Onalaska, Kalama, Vader, and all the places people live south of Seattle—have their stories and folks and families; their creatures and legends and lore. What they don't automatically come with is a muse. How fortunate the village inhabited by the likes of a LeMonds, skilled in the telling his people's stories and incapable of holding them in.

A couple of years ago, Jim began sending drafts of his essays our way. I'd met him, liked him, and found him articulate and caring. Like any writer, I receive a lot of manuscripts, and I was a little slow on the uptake. But I liked what I read, and Thea (my own best editor-of-first-recourse) devoured them with obvious pleasure. Clearly, in between his celebrated high-school English teaching and his family devotions, Jim was building a book of this place. Soon, we both realized that these portraits and lessons needed sharing. When it came clear that Mountain Press was going to bring out *South of Seattle*, a cheer went up from K.O. Peak to Baw Faw Peak and resounded through the damp valleys all the way to Mount St. Helens.

When you take this trip, you will enter a town that has changed less than many places but more than anyone in it could have imagined. You will find out about small-town, and how that waning situation still has virtue in these amalgamating times. How the riches of rain may take you unawares, as your palette of greens grows wildly. How country graveyards indict the mythlessness of the present as they flesh out the corpus of the heretofore; how a personal geography can snap and process instant prints of the past; how the trees have come and gone and left behind a ruined architecture, come and gone again, and again—these are the routes of whim and wisdom you'll travel in the territory ahead. The getting in of firewood, the pulling-in at autumn, the hunt, and hunter-dog Coyote; the eruption and rebirth at nearby St. Helens, the loss and lessons of a compatriot almost forgotten, and a "Scripture for the Land" that takes it all in—even smelt. Such are the gifts to be found, after all, *South of Seattle*.

Before this volume, my *Wintergreen* was about the only book of personal essay mined from the leached soils and logged-off land of the Willapa country. A mutual friend, when he heard of this book's imminent arrival, asked if I minded sharing the literary turf. Fair question. But I had to laugh: when you think of all the lenses that have been trained on the Olympics, the Cascades, and the Sierra, not to mention the Adirondacks, the Appalachians, or the Allegheny; and then reflect that no range's story is ever adequately told, let alone exhausted, you can imagine that another book on my little corner of the West (from the other side of the hills, yet!) can only be a source of delight and anticipation. Especially a good book. And this *is* a good book. Jim LeMonds is one of those rare and lucky writers with "a heart that hunts the landscape's story." Here, way south of Seattle, he has found it.

ROBERT MICHAEL PYLE

Robert Michael Pyle is the author of *Wintergreen*, *The Thunder Tree*, *Where Bigfoot Walks*, and a bunch of butterfly books. He lives somewhere west of Skamokawa.

Preface

*"Tell me the landscape in which you live,
and I will tell you who you are."*
                                    —Jose Ortega y Gasset

WE ARE SMALL-TOWN AND NOT INCLINED TO APOLOGIZE FOR IT. Life in places like ours, the grainy-edged, pin-dot burghs of America, is bonded like a weld to a set of shared tales and elastic truths, geographic guideposts and myopic myths that lose their viability once the county line has been crossed. Ours is a Yoknapatawpha of our own making, a place with color and coherence, where the fact that people know your name is not a bad thing but a comfort, like a frayed afghan worn in the evenings to ward off the chill.

There is more give-and-take in small towns, and mine is no exception. Here, people know about your ups and downs, about your past and your present. They know your grandparents, your children, the house you grew up in, and the names of places too tiny to be listed on any map. Only in a small town will people understand when you tell them that so-and-so bought the old Kettewig place, that you saw deer cross the highway near Mickey Mouse, or that springers are hitting on flatfish down at the Preacher Hole. We are woven together, threads in a fabric of shared stories, language, and geography. While never wholly liberated from the rumor-mongering, petty jealousies, and tiresome expectations of our neighbors, we accept the trade-off as currency well spent in a place where knowing is closely related to belonging.

Welcome to Castle Rock and the Maritime Northwest. This is the land of contradiction, the place of promise and despair, of staggering wildness and unthrottled development, of Bigfoot and Bill Gates, of ancient forests and endless clear-cuts, of small-town hospitality and redneck repartee, of salmon as fact and salmon as fable. This is the Far Corner, where dreams grow green and plump, and the road can still take you home, provided you know the way.

South of Seattle

AST FROM THE I-5 CORRIDOR, ridges hoist themselves from the valleys, fold into mountains, and pile like cloud banks to the edge of the sky. Across the distance, the landscape changes color: green fades to hazy navy and then to cobalt on the lip of the horizon. Undulations give way to angles, sharpening to form the jagged peaks of the Cascades. Twenty-five million years old, the range extends 700 miles from Shasta in northern California up through Oregon and Washington and into British Columbia. Hood, Adams, St. Helens, Rainier, and Baker are its showpieces, volcanic peaks less than a million years old strung like claymore mines through one of the most active chains in the world.

Ascending to form the eastern border of the Maritime Northwest, the Cascades are the region's most significant geographic feature, wringing moisture from the jet stream as clouds, fat with Pacific rain, rise to clear them. Dozens of rivers—among them the Skagit, Skykomish, Stillaguamish, Nisqually, Nooksack, Cowlitz, Toutle, Kalama, Lewis—spring in the mountains and find their way to Puget Sound or the Columbia, carrying the runoff from the Cascades in a land dominated by water and green.

Forty miles west of Mt. St. Helens, the timber community of Castle Rock (pronounced "Cassa Rock" by the locals) sits like a comfortable old dog between the Cowlitz River and Interstate 5 at the easternmost edge of the Willapa Hills. We are two hours south of Seattle, one hour north of Portland, seven miles west of Toutle, and a half-mile east of Four Corners. If we are supposed to be waiting for something, few of us could tell you what it is.

I live three miles west of town on Growlers Gulch Road. The name has forced me into countless explanations for clerks and secretaries and other officials for whom addresses are essential business. They smile and tease good-naturedly, probably bestowing country bumpkin status on me in the process. I haven't found anyone who is certain how the moniker originated, though I've spent more than a few hours considering the possibilities. Was there, perhaps, a group of growly gulch dwellers who at one time did battle over property lines with words and fists? Or does the name refer to the grumble of car and truck engines shifted down for the winding climb up the hills toward Weyerhaeuser country? Better that it remain a mystery.

Admittedly, our road system on the Gulch is a bit out of the ordinary. Imagine a one-lane road with a line painted down the middle to create the illusion that two lanes exist and you have the picture. It's fine when a Karmann Ghia meets a bicycle, but it is not a suitable place for a car to encounter a log truck swinging wide to make a corner, Jake brake screaming for you to aim your rig for the ditch or risk serious injury. If the weather is just wrong, there is a better-than-average chance the big culvert that carries the Arkansas Creek under the road will clog with debris and rise up to submerge the pavement. While the county crew usually has things cleaned up before long, you can get home the back way if you're in a rush, provided you're willing to take your chances on a logging-road detour.

Some days, traffic is delayed for a moment if two people have stopped their cars, rolled down their windows, and struck up a conversation, or if Harvey Anderson has parked his tractor in the middle of the road while he attends to some errand in an adjacent field. Harvey lives at the bottom of the hill just as you wind down into the Gulch. He is the owner of what I refer to as the "Barn of Black Humor." White letters five feet high made of one-by-fours and tacked against the red barn spell "HA". Certainly one could explain it by saying that these are Harvey's initials, this is his barn, and it makes perfect sense for him to attach letters to it. But I've never believed it was that simple. Harvey has endured for a good part of the century and has seen life from every angle. Perhaps those two letters are his dark response to all that he has witnessed, like a dispossessed refrain muttered by some beaten-down antihero in a Kurt Vonnegut novel.

Traffic problems and nihilistic barns are a small price to pay for privacy and friendliness, however. We wave to people out our way, even if we don't know them. And if you need a hand, someone like Jim and Audrey Dunbar will be there to lend one. Several years ago, while my wife and I were vacationing in Montana, our daughter Kim was on her way to a job in Kelso when her pickup broke down in front of the Dunbars' home. Jim pushed the pickup out of the road, and Audrey made a twenty-five-mile round trip to get Kim to work on time. Sherry baked them a cake as a thank-you, but they didn't expect a reward. They just did what good people do.

There are plenty of folks like Jim and Audrey in the Castle Rock area. Raised on hard work and a strong measure of self-sufficiency, they are partial to plain talk and sound hearts. They are sustained by a landscape as raw and unpretentious as the old-timers who first settled here. Although I am considerably more rabid than my neighbors about the need to salvage what remains of wild spaces and species, we share both a love for what Robert Michael Pyle so eloquently dubbed this "wintergreen world" and a belief that ours is the finest corner of the planet. You can lodge complaints against the weather and bemoan the lack of things cosmopolitan, but once you have been seduced, once you are rooted, the grip is like a manacle, and thoughts of leaving soon rise and drift east on the jet stream.

In 1852, William and Eliza Huntington came west from Illinois on the Oregon Trail. They lost two of their children to cholera on the way. When they reached what is now southwest Washington, the river-bottom land in the Cowlitz Valley had already been staked out from present-day Longview north to Lexington. The Huntingtons traveled six miles upriver to distance themselves from the other homesteaders and filed a 299-acre donation land claim along the Cowlitz near a cathedral-size chunk of basalt that local rivermen referred to as "Castle Rock." William Huntington formally named the town and established a post office. At various times, he served as U.S. marshal, postmaster, and member of the Territorial House of Representatives and Senate.

I've seen a grainy 1920s photo of the Rock, taken from the west side of the river looking east. In the picture, it is squatty, bare, and unimpressive, something like a free-form paperweight sculpted by a nephew in the Cub Scouts. The city owns the property now, and the only development is a shady trail to the top, edged with ferns and salmonberry. I remember making the journey with my classmates on a spring day when I was in first grade. Mrs. Faulk led us down Huntington Avenue, lunch pails in hand, and we meandered up the Rock, searching for spring beauties and Johnny-jump-ups. Thirty-six years later, I retraced our route and found that little had changed.

The ground was damp with the previous day's rain. Flies and mosquitoes floated from the brush in search of blood. A robin skittered through a tangle of sword ferns and berry vines just off the trail, perhaps in an attempt to lead me away from her young. I stopped to search but was unable to find them. At the top, ivy crept through the underbrush and climbed like leggings more than a hundred feet up several second-growth firs and cedars that have been here since the Rock was logged in the 1920s. The trail led to the crumbling cement remains of the old city water tank that crouches atop the hill like a World War II bunker. Through the leaves and boughs the Cowlitz River lay 200 feet below, shimmering and green in the early evening shade.

From across the channel, the chatter of fishermen relaxing in lawn chairs on the gravel bar rose to me like the conversations of neighbors in yards down the block. I imagined they were the voices of the Huntington children, playing along the river, skipping stones and dangling their feet in the Cowlitz while their parents sat in the shade and spoke in intimate tones, revisiting stories of friends and family left behind and wondering if the Midwest was getting its usual dose of thunderstorms and humidity.

When the Northern Pacific Railroad laid down tracks from Kalama to Tacoma in the 1870s, Castle Rock found itself on the main line. As the town began to grow, it was logged with oxen and eventually incorporated in 1890. Because Castle Rock was a frontier community with an attitude to match, things were predictably rough: the logbook of the local justice of the peace noted a fistfight on virtually every day of the year. A log jail was built, but the fine art of incarceration got off to a rocky start when Hanaman Haywood became the jail's first prisoner and its first escapee. Paid by the city to build the structure, Haywood had installed a particularly roomy chimney in the event he should ever find himself imprisoned in his own creation. His capture and subsequent conviction for jailbreak followed the escape quite shortly. A few years later, the city contracted with Al Rosin to construct a new jail. He used concrete, and neither Hanaman Haywood nor anyone else ever got out of that one.

Jim Price, who was the marshal in 1905, was a well-known figure, viewed less than enthusiastically by those convicted of crimes. Price made a habit of staking prisoners out with a ball and chain along city streets where they grubbed stumps, qualifying Castle Rock's penal system as one of the Northwest's first to simultaneously provide rehabilitation, civic development, vocational training, and aerobic exercise.

River-bottom land in the valley was rich, and crops grew well. They were shipped by steamboat down the Cowlitz to the Columbia, then to Oregon, California, or Hawaii. However, the big money in the area at the turn of the century was generated by the shingle industry. Upriver on the Cowlitz and the Toutle, red cedar logs the diameter of missile silos were bucked into fifty-six-inch sections, split in half to make them easier to handle, and floated to mills in Castle Rock, where they were cut into shakes. According to local historian Leland Jackson, a popular and sometimes deadly stunt for area kids was to jump into the river upstream and ride the shingle bolts to town, a rite of passage that claimed several lives each year.

The shingle business brought jobs, people, and the construction of a downtown area. A number of hotels sprang up within walking distance of the mills. But by the mid-1920s the red cedar had gone the way of the passenger pigeon, and the boom period was over. Construction in the few blocks that now comprise downtown Castle Rock soon came to a halt, and there have been few structures erected since then. The American Legion now meets in what was once the Savoy Hotel. The Pastime Tavern occupies the old Hille Drug Store. The concrete jail built by Al Rosin is no longer in use, but hunkers with the resilience of a cedar stump on Jackson Street between Cascade Market and the Baptist church.

When I was growing up during the '50s and '60s, the post office was located on First Street where Ken Davis now has the Castle Rock Pharmacy. In the entryway was a sign—"No Calk Boots Allowed"—put there to protect the wood floor. Calks (pronounced "corks") are work boots with short spikes in the soles, similar to those found on golf shoes, which enable loggers to walk on downed timber without slipping. The fact that the sign was necessary says a great deal about the flavor of the community. It was and is a town dominated by loggers and logging, millworkers and working-class families looking for a chance to raise their kids in a place where gunfire is relegated to hunting season.

In the 1930s and 1940s, most loggers lived out of town in camps up the Toutle Valley toward Mt. St. Helens. On Friday nights, Weyerhaeuser hooked coaches behind the locomotives and brought the men into Castle Rock and Kelso for the weekend. Rigging slingers, chasers, hooktenders, donkey punchers, fallers, and climbers, they rode into town like range cowboys to blow off steam, do a little drinking, and search for romance. They duded up, maybe in pressed white shirt, felt hat, and dress shoes, but at the very least in a new hickory shirt and overalls. On Saturday nights they hung around the Washington Barbershop, owned and operated by Fred Roller and Ed Rosin on the corner of Cowlitz and Front, where a man could get a hot bath, a shoeshine, a shave, and a haircut.

Hard liquor wasn't sold by the individual drink in those days, so the loggers bought fifths of whiskey and stashed them in the back of the barbershop. When they stopped in for a drink during the evening, part of the arrangement was that Fred Roller was entitled to a nip—sort of a service charge for storing the booze. Occasionally, it led to some very crooked haircuts. The men would stand on the corner and talk, hit the Pastime or the Oasis Tavern for a beer, or check out the weekly dance above Hanson and Becker's General Store. There were plenty of fights, and Sheriff Pritchard had his share of drunk-and-disorderlies to contend with.

The camps are gone now—work crews ride to the woods in buses called "crummies" or in king-cab pickups—and Castle Rock is a quiet place, even on weekends. We've become a bedroom community of Longview, where Fibre, Weyerhaeuser, Reynolds Metals, and Norpac offer the type of high-dollar jobs that are fading from the American industrial landscape. The theater where I watched *The Blob* as a boy is boarded up, and there are no longer any clothing stores in town that can compete with the attraction of the mall just down the freeway in Kelso. Life sails along pretty much the same from day to day. We are huddled near the stove with our feet up and the quilt pulled around our shoulders.

Castle Rock has nine churches, three taverns, a Speedy Mart, grocery, hardware store, pharmacy, flower shop, variety store, several automotive businesses, a saw shop, a handful of restaurants, and some fine people who know the value of family and friendship. It's not Grover's Corners, but it could be your town, or just about any town.

We aren't much for fashion trendiness. It's true that plenty of people wear plaid shirts, but that has considerably less to do with trying to mimic the Seattle grunge scene than it does with a legacy of durable work wear left by Pendleton and Filsun. We haven't been wholly able to escape the flow of culture surging down the interstate from Seattle, however. The Northwest is coffee country, and espresso has come to town. Although I'm an admitted addict, I must confess to a bit of disappointment. It's hard to reconcile the image of millworkers and burly loggers in suspenders and stagged-off overalls with words like cappuccino and latte. But espresso is here, and not just at some yuppie coffee shop, but at the Cascade Market, the Texaco, the Speedy Mart, and, of all places, the Mexican take-out joint. My taste buds have not yet come to grips with the idea of combining a mocha with a burrito and an order of Mexi-fries.

We aren't noted for anything earth-shattering—other than the eruption of Mt. St. Helens—and it's difficult for us to assume much credit for that, or for the three million tourists who take Exit 49 east of town each year and motor up Spirit Lake Highway, hoping for one of those rare days when visibility cooperates and they are able to glimpse the remains of the mountain.

We do have a modest hall of fame that includes some people whose names might be recognized beyond the reaches of the Cowlitz Valley. Arnold Reigger won truckloads of medals as a trapshooter, bringing back national titles and earning a spot in the 1960 Olympics as a member of the U.S. trapshooting team. Tom Hansen graduated from Castle Rock High in the '50s and, for a few years, wrote the sports column for the local paper, the *Cowlitz County Advocate*; today he's commissioner of the Pacific-10 Athletic Conference. And we like to brag about Hap Johnson. If the name doesn't ring any bells, check out a copy of *North to Alaska* from your video store. When John Wayne races up those trees with his spurs and climbing belt, you'll see that Hap Johnson was one hell of a climber—sixteen times a world tree-topping champ—and a damn good double as well. Hap became our first media star when he made several national television appearances in the late '50s and early '60s. He performed at a road show hosted by Arthur Godfrey and filmed at Shelton, Washington, where he showed off his talents in climbing, topping, bucking, and ax throwing. He also guest-starred on Art Baker's "You Asked for It," putting on a display that wowed both host and audience. I remember watching that show, eager to see a local hero get his due. Despite my initial excitement, I was left with a discomfort that I couldn't explain. Years later, I realized that Hap had been displayed like a rawboned country ball player at a Rose Garden ceremony. It marked my initial realization that we have a strong sense of place that does not always transplant well.

Since the late 1960s the local motorcycle club has kept us on the map, sponsoring regional weekend races and even pulling in a national tourist trophy event that attracts the big names in the cycle world and upwards of 10,000 fans. Initially, people feared the Banditos or the Hell's Angels might come tooling into town for a weekend of riot and destruction. But instead of Sonny Berger on a chopper with a twelve-over rake, kicked back against the sissy bar of his solo seat, we've mainly attracted dentists and accountants, cruising on their "dressers," Harley FXH-1200s with luggage carriers on the sides. It's a slight letdown for those of us who grew up watching *Easy Rider*.

We have the typical small-town crime—domestic violence, theft, drunk-and-disorderly—and the drug trade seeping outward from urban America has begun to show its face here. People no longer leave their doors unlocked at night, but most go to bed feeling secure. Assaults and shootings related to traffic trauma are rare in Castle Rock, since we have very little traffic. We do boast flashing lights that announce all-way stops at the intersections of Huntington and Cowlitz and Huntington and A, but most people would say they are without serious purpose, other than to trumpet the fact that we are indeed a city.

When I left for Western Washington University in Bellingham in 1968, I had lived my first eighteen years in Castle Rock. I had joined the Cub Scouts, played Little League baseball, tied a bath towel around my neck and attempted to fly like Superman from the top step of my neighbor's porch, and explored every inch of the Jim Town neighborhood where I grew up. From the time I was eight until I was thirteen, I biked the mile to town most summer days when the community pool was open. After cooling off at the afternoon swimming session, I visited the library located upstairs in what is now the city hall in search of new adventure novels featuring my heroes: the Hardy Boys, Chip Hilton, and Tom Swift. And maybe once a week I'd walk on the wild side, charging a ten-cent ice cream sandwich at the Mercantile, where Wendell Dougherty and Floyd Punches kept handwritten tabs in rowed cubbyholes behind the counter and the wood floors oozed a sweet balm of welcome as mellow and inclusive as the proprietors themselves.

I attended the local high school, played football and basketball, fell in and out of love a couple of times, took the requisite stabs at manhood armed with six-packs of Rainier and a 327 V-8, and somehow convinced myself I wanted to teach seventh-grade social studies. Those years at college put a great distance between Castle Rock and myself. By the time I was a junior, I was a markedly different person from the boy in a crewcut who, believing that American foreign policy was comparable to holy writ, had used his high school graduation speech to deliver a rousing denunciation of communist imperialism in Asia. I had grown my hair out, listened to Ralph Nader, seen Tina Turner live, learned to play a little Dylan on the guitar, drunk my share of keg beer, marched in antiwar rallies, and helped block Interstate 5 when the U.S. invaded Cambodia. I was worldly-wise, and there was no way I was going back to a place without a bookstore, where the highlight of a Friday evening was a burger at C&L.

Or so I thought. While attending Western, I met Sherry and took the biggest and best fall of my life. We married at the end of my junior year and decided that when I graduated we would accept a teaching job wherever one was offered. I applied at Long Beach, California; Mount Vernon, Washington; and just about every place in between. As fate would have it, I was offered a position teaching social studies and English at Cascade Junior High in Longview, just ten minutes south of Castle Rock. We were excited to have a job, but I had serious reservations about returning. I believed Thomas Wolfe was at least partially right: it wasn't so much that you couldn't go home, it was just better that you didn't.

That was twenty-three years ago. We rented a house in Castle Rock near the freeway for a year or two, then began work on the home on Growlers Gulch where we now live. For the first ten years, I was embarrassed to be back. I'd gone to college to become something more than a small-town boy who drank beer at the Oasis and walked the sidelines at high school football games. I talked of moving to Eugene or Bellingham or Olympia, places where art and music and diversity were more accessible. But something held me. Initially, I believed it was merely an unwillingness to endure the inconvenience of changing jobs and moving my family. With time, I began to understand that I have stayed because I am anchored here by history and love, and because there is a coherence in this part of the universe that I refuse to relinquish.

Perhaps the onset of middle age was helpful in erasing my concerns about what others might think. Or maybe I simply realized that this place is my place and that no apologies need be made.

On a lazy Saturday morning not long ago, Sherry and I lay in bed after coffee and lovemaking. Less than forty feet from our bedroom window, five deer nibbled on the plum trees: two yearlings; a three-point buck, its antlers still in velvet; and a doe with a spotted fawn, which pranced up the driveway with the innocence and arrogance of a child, glancing over its shoulder occasionally to make certain that mom approved. When I opened the front door and stepped onto the porch, the buck posed for me like a bored uncle at a family reunion.

Now that I am willing to acknowledge the richness of life in this landscape, I have set out to tabulate the treasures I had once been willing to exchange for things urbane: the eave of my house does not threaten to touch that of my neighbor; hummingbirds dart and pause among potted marigolds on the deck; towhees and finches and Steller's jays chatter in the bird feeders; coyotes howl from across the canyon; crickets play for each other as they have for 220 million years. On silent indigo nights, the clatter of the train in the valley five miles east drifts through my bedroom window like the gentle passing of a night creature. It is comfortable as a well-worn sweatshirt.

For now, Castle Rock has escaped the phenomenal growth that spurts like an open artery south from Puget Sound and north from Portland. Our population has held steady at just over 2,000 for several decades, but dramatic change is on the way. Experts predict that Washington's population will increase by 50 percent in the next quarter-century, with an additional five million people expected to spill into the Northwest by the year 2020. The region permanently loses more than 100,000 acres of forest land annually to development, as we feed the voracious demand for sprawling tracts of affordable property to be used for housing and commercial construction. Nearly 70 percent of the wetlands in the Puget Sound area are gone. Eighty percent of the state's old-growth forest has been cut. Dams block more than half of Washington's salmon streams. In the Columbia Basin, native fish runs have declined by as much as 98 percent. In 1995, one salmon returned to spawn at Salmon, Idaho.

As what passes for progress presses in, we are left to consider what it means to live "a good life" and what role landscape will play in determining the value of the existence we have long taken for granted. Oddly, the deterioration adds relish to my days. I am aware of what I have and what my children stand to lose. I hold tight to every sunrise and cloudburst, to the shadowy flutter of maple leaves and the surprise of elk in a field along Westside Highway on my drive to work.

I often walk the road to a knoll at the end of a gravel spur, where on a clear day you can see Rainier, St. Helens, Adams, and 220 degrees of blue-green horizon. I look down to where Castle Rock scatters in the river bottom and remind myself that I was born in this valley, that I have spent all but four years of my life here, and that in all probability it is where I will die and be buried.

Being rooted has little to do with latitude and longitude, the variables that follow the hyphen in a zip code, or the size of the local phone book. It is simply a matter of how well you know your place and how comfortably you fit there. I have become what Wendell Berry called a "placed person," and I no longer resent it. It is the ultimate affirmation that this is my home.

Easter Morning

I N A MOTEL LOBBY IN BELLINGHAM, WASHINGTON, at dawn on Easter morning, unable to sleep, I drink coffee and read Terry Tempest Williams's book *An Unspoken Hunger*. Muscular clouds dominate the sky, their undersides streaked with black. A fine mist is falling, but the day will likely bring real rain. To the south, the interstate slides away toward the horizon like a sleek gray stream. The drive home promises congestion and near-zero visibility, navigation better suited to a pilot able to make his way on instruments alone.

A stumpy older woman engages the desk clerk in a conversation he doesn't want. The woman and her husband are visiting the Northwest from Arizona, and all she can do is complain about the weather. "Our friends from Seattle always tell us how lovely it is here," she says, "but I think *lousy* is a better word. We went to bed last night hoping for a pretty Easter. I don't mind telling you, we were very disappointed when we woke up to this mess." She waves an accusing hand in the general direction of the floor-to-ceiling windows that reveal the mess, as if expecting the desk clerk to rescue the day. "How do you people stand this rain? It is so depressing." She moves off to survey the continental breakfast, still talking to the uninterested clerk, turning her criticism from the malevolent weather to her tardy husband, who will make them late for Easter services.

Unable to tear herself away from the sweet rolls, she is blind to the surrounding hills, swollen with life sprung from the rain that animates this land. Winter has retreated, and the landscape is potent and lush. The cottonwoods' chartreuse plumage is muted in the gray of morning, but one ray of light will show it to be electric against the navy green of Douglas fir and cedar. Swales of alder, their leaves no bigger than thumbnails, have not yet decided whether to be green or gray. Everywhere there is budding and bursting to leaf as liquid life is sucked from the ground and squeezed out the tips of branches.

The Native Americans of the Pacific Northwest believed that people in arid climates had been sentenced by the Great Spirit to parched lives devoid of moisture. Long ago, according to legend, those who lived in dry lands asked Ocean to send his children, Rain and Cloud, to bring the moisture that would make their land bloom and the streams run with fish. Ocean heeded their request and the wishes of the dry-lands people were granted, but when he asked that his children be allowed to return, the people of the desert refused to let Rain and Cloud go. Ocean carried his sorrow to the Great Spirit, who took back the moisture from the dry-lands people as retribution for their selfishness and cruelty; from that day forward, he granted rainfall only to those nearest to his heart. There are, of course, those, like the woman from Arizona, who doubt the legend, and scientists have explanations of their own.

The record for rainfall during a twelve-month period in the forty-eight contiguous states was established in Washington at Big Four Camp, on the western edge of the Cascades. Between March 9, 1931, and March 5, 1932, precipitation totaled 203.56 inches. Outsiders would be surprised to learn, however, that western Washington averages much less than that—about thirty-five to forty inches of rain a year, with nearly half of it concentrated in the winter months. We are recipients of what meteorologists refer to as orographic rainfall. The jet stream pushes storms in from the Pacific, forcing them across the Olympics and Cascades, where colder temperatures reduce the air's capacity to hold water vapor, resulting in the rain that inundates and defines us. From December through March, "partly cloudy with a chance of rain" is a forecast so certain that weathermen have little function. People who believe moisture is a curse don't stay long. Those who remain are privy to blessings seldom granted elsewhere.

The theorem is simple: no rain, no wintergreen; no white water, no salmon. Nothing would grow without the forced hand of irrigation. No moss. No bracken fern. No forest rife with life-forms beyond imagination. No sense that the land itself is set to erupt with life and green.

Silent a moment, the woman pours herself a cup of coffee and picks a corner off a maple bar. She isn't interested in hearing it, but the matter is a plain one on this Easter morning in the Northwest: without rain there can be no rebirth.

Northwest Dreaming

Y DECEMBER 1936, MY GRANDFATHER'S CAREER as a Midwest tenant farmer had fallen victim to dust storms and economic depression. The LeMondses were not precisely the Joads of Steinbeck's *The Grapes of Wrath,* but the comparison is there if you are so inclined. That winter, Bill LeMonds took a hard look at the 200 acres of frozen Iowa farmland he'd leased near Malvern and decided the time had come to leave the region where he had spent his entire life. He sold the livestock and the farm equipment, loaded the family's clothing, dishes, and bedding into his 1935 Chevy pickup and a 1930 Oldsmobile that belonged to his son Bob, and headed for the Promised Land of the Pacific Northwest.

They spent that Christmas in a tourist camp—a motel with cooking facilities; travelers supplied their own food and utensils—in The Dalles, Oregon. When they rolled into Vancouver two days later, my father was sixteen. He has told me the story of their exodus many times. The details change occasionally, but when I called him this week, fifty-eight years after the fact, to ask about the incident, no prompting was necessary to summon the impression that remains rooted in his mind like a primal dream: "She sure looked good when we came down the Gorge and into Vancouver. We'd crossed 2,000 miles of ice and snow and all of a sudden everything was so damn green."

Someone once asked a friend of mine why he'd moved to Longview, Washington, from his native Montana. "It was all that green," he replied. "I'd never seen anything like it." Although my friend has since returned to Missoula, his words echo with uncanny precision the thoughts of my father nearly five decades earlier. There is so much of it that our senses seem unwilling to take us beyond the simplistic description I have heard from my friend, my father, and many, many others: *It is just so damn green.*

Try to picture green and a limited range of color will appear. Be prepared for an expansion of that palette when your eyes open to the greens of the Maritime Northwest. They are a powerful, pervasive force, defying simple classification, traversing a spectrum and defining a region, seeping into the heart and the mind's eye.

The jet stream rarely forgets us, sweeping up moisture in the northern Pacific and tossing inland a cycle of storms that lay down sheets of rainfall as they climb the staggered ridges on their way toward the Cascades. Through winter and spring, rain soaks the ground until a walk across your lawn can be like a trek across a great soggy sponge. Moisture rises from the earth, not just as condensation, but in the blades and needles, leaves and blossoms, stalks and trunks of foliage that run up their festive flags of green. Allegiance can wane in the face of so much gray and damp; those who are unable to deal with it make their way south or east to climes where slugs and dry rot have no hold. But for those who remain, green's fecund embrace is our payment for enduring rain and overcast that seem determined to rule the sky from November through the front edge of summer.

You can travel the route between Vancouver and Castle Rock that my father's family took so many years ago as they searched for jobs and a place they could adopt as their own. Or select your own destination and mode of transportation: virtually any locale west of the Cascades will do. The hills lie before you like the gift of a magician who has worked her spells for untold millennia, tinting even the rivers green with the borrowed reflection of the trees.

Throughout the year, green is held in fir and cedar and wild grass, but in April and May the world of rain is transformed into a variegated tribute to the color in innumerable hues and shades. Spring in the Northwest can make you a believer in the miracle of photosynthesis, not as a theory set forth in science texts, but as a process you can physically witness: the capturing of light in leaf, an ocular buzz of intensity as sunlight reveals that it is sun life.

In early April, maple announces itself in a show of thalo green, delicate flowers hanging from branches like Japanese lanterns, harbingers of leaves that will retain a distinct reminder of yellow when they soften to match the radiant green of huckleberry. Where cottonwoods grow along the stream banks, the explosion comes in chartreuse that outshines even maple. But unlike maple, cottonwood sees the future, its leaves holding a drop of ochre that hints of the orange that September and October will bring.

From a distance, alder hazes and dulls. Muted beside the glow of maple, it is the green of weathered bridges. A closer look reveals that alder carries a touch of sunlight in leaves that blend with the undergrowth hidden beneath the canopy of conifer and broadleaf: cascading mounds of evergreen and Himalayan blackberry vines; bleeding heart; salmonberry; fireweed; dogwood with its creamy button-blossoms; wild cherry; fuzzy hazel; stinging nettle, whose Velcro leaves in August will snatch the airborne puffball seeds of thistle and tansy; vine maple with leaves of electric lemon-green; the ungainly arcs of elderberry, its foliage capped with spires delicate as baby's-breath; sword ferns the color of martini olives; dark, melon-rind green of waxy salal and Oregon grape; moss that clings to alder and maple, green as billiard cloth in the shade but tinged umber where sunlight wields its wand.

On road banks and in clearings, Scotch broom sprouts foliage of deep mint that will go unnoticed in May, when it wears blooms bright as summer squash. Grass provides a plush accent, tempering the open ugliness of clear-cuts and spilling across the landscape without regard for season.

Conifers grow here so heartily that some consider them a crop. Among them, cedar is most frequently associated with warmth. Cedar is not long-burning, but on December evenings its flames pop and flare a fireplace invitation to curl up with a book or a loved one. Cedar's boughs droop slightly to catch the sun's glow, the tips of its fronds tinged with suggestions of gold as it joins the broadleafs in celebration.

Ultimately, however, it is forest green you must dream when you are in the Maritime Northwest. Douglas firs and hemlocks sponge up light, draining brightness to blackish green when the sun is hidden or when dusk arrives. Their limbs reach up like the blades of scimitars, undersides drawing off the green and fusing a blue brooding to the hills. They are drought resistant, accustomed to long summer dry spells and equipped to photosynthesize year-round. Clear-cuts have taken their toll, but the firs this land is known for still roll dark green to the horizons in quiet contrast to the puffed spring plumage of broadleaf, reminding us in a voice diminished by time and destruction that this evergreen place is a gift they have chosen to share.

In *Wintergreen,* Robert Michael Pyle makes clear what is transitory and what is permanent in the Maritime Northwest: "When the mills close, the log trucks stop rolling, the dairies go to summer beef or weeds, the fresh, wet green remains the same." My father refuses to return to the Midwest, even for a visit to the old home place. Green is part of the lushness and abundance that have rooted him here as firmly as a Douglas fir. He is woven into the fabric of the land and the color that claims it, and neither he nor the green is willing to let go.

Voices from the Old World

OWER CEMETERY LIES ADJACENT to a twisting two-lane road four miles east of Castle Rock. I have come today to visit the place where my mother's people now reside. The dream they followed carried them 8,000 miles from hearth and home to the Cowlitz River Valley, and finally here, to an unassuming one-acre plot where a good portion of my history is kept. Theirs was the quintessential American dream of freedom and opportunity, and it shone as brightly as the stars of Orion.

The cemetery is as humble as its inhabitants. The low end borders the road, then eases up the hill to a meager backdrop of fir, cedar, and alder. Beyond the barbed-wire fence that forms the northern border of the cemetery, the yellow eyes of March daffodils peer at me suspiciously. Intruders are rare, especially those with paper and pen.

The flavor is Old World and decidedly German. The headstones carry the names my mother spoke when I was a boy: Berndt, Janisch, Roller, Rosin, Stankey. They crossed the Atlantic on tickets sent by brothers and sisters who had scrimped and saved to pay the passage. Perhaps there was a stopover in the German communities of the Great Lakes region, where they could try the New World on and test the fit. Eventually, they were pulled west to Washington by family connections, the promise of jobs, or a climate that evoked images of home. Many of them settled along Tower Road, where throaty German brogue and the pungent aroma of sauerkraut invited belonging. They attended

St. Paul's Lutheran Church in Castle Rock, holding to their beliefs as stubbornly as to their property lines. If you'd had occasion to ask them about their final resting place, they would have told you bluntly that Tower Cemetery would lay claim only to their bodies; their souls were the property of God the Father. Because I am less sure about the Place of Souls than they were, I take Walt Whitman's suggestion and search for them in the grass beneath my boot heels.

I had expected a thick carpet of fairway green, but the grass is brown and sparse, choked out by moss and weeds. Moles make headway where they can. The ground is uneven, settling as the earth folds the bodies back within itself. The sexton has been here, filling low spots with sod and loose dirt.

Church records say that in 1907 Ida Kroll was the first to be buried in Tower Cemetery, but I have been unable to find her stone. There are others whose places are unmarked, and once the final settling that reveals their presence is finished, they will have truly completed the circle from dust to dust. The erasure takes place more slowly here than at the seashore, but time will eventually claim even the headstones. Tenuous and temporary, they are merely a different type of footprint in the sand.

As is often the case, husbands have preceded their wives. My uncle, Bill Strain, holds a place for Aunt Selma. Johnnie Franstvog has waited here for Emma since 1978. For the time being, the Brockmans, Carl and Marian, live across the road, but their place has already been set in marble. Smoke trails from their chimney like the leavings of an old man's pipe, rolls up the pasture, and hangs in the firs that top the hill. The Brockman family has lived in that house for sixty-five years. It will be a short journey from there to here.

Plastic geraniums brighten a few graves, but the most appropriate decoration is the faded red carnation left for infant Katherine Downing, a cousin I will never know. She lies beside her brother Greg. He was thirty-two when his body gave up the fight against the debilitation that followed a swimming accident that left him paralyzed for a decade. I remember him as a scrappy seventh-grade point guard, his energy boundless, his future seemingly without limits. Wildflowers held together by a bread sack twister are his boutonniere.

The Kluths have carried the Old Country with them in their names: Mathilde, Edmund, Erna, Adolf, Ewald, Selma, Gustaf. They are comfortable near the Weinheimers, whose headstones have weathered the color and texture of wet sand. Edward Weinheimer was eighteen years old when he died in 1917. A lamb, now fleeced with lichen, rests above the inscription: *Ruhe sanft in Deiner Gruft. Bis Dich einst Dein Heiland ruft. Repose softly in your grave, til your savior calls you.* That admonition has been heeded. Parents Jakob and Louise lie nearby, united by a marker that reads, *Der Herr ist unser Hirte, uns wird nichts mangeln. The Lord is our shepherd, we shall not want.* I trace the words with my fingers and think of the Rosetta Stone: mysterious symbols feebly attempting to speak of lives.

Albert Rosin Senior and his wife, Pauline, share a headstone that tilts noticeably in Pauline's direction. A tiny crucifix links their names. Albert was born in Swanteestolp, Germany, in 1862 and died in Castle Rock in 1939. He came to America through Canada in 1884 and found work on a section crew in Sault St. Marie, Michigan, where he met brothers Ferdinand and Gustav Stankey. Albert was a bachelor searching for a wife, so the Stankeys suggested their sister, Pauline, who was living in England. They sent word to her, and the match was made. On the night he and Pauline were married in July 1889, Albert danced holes in the soles of his shoes. The Rosins moved west just after the turn of the century, and the Stankeys soon followed. Because Castle Rock had no Lutheran church, Albert pledged $500 toward the construction of one. Later, he deeded to that same church one acre of his farm on Tower Road for this cemetery, so that his friends from the Old Country, separated by an ocean from their ancestors, would have a suitable place to spend eternity.

Albert Rosin Junior died in France on October 12, 1918, thirty days before the armistice. He had been drafted into the 20th Corps of Engineers, who were looking for men with road-building skills and logging experience. Albert Senior had planned to give his son the family farm in Olequa when he returned from the war, but halfway around the globe from where you would expect a logging accident to occur, Albert Rosin Junior was killed when a log swung by a boom machine crushed him against a stump. *Christus ist mein Leben. Sterben ist mein Gewinn,* they wrote on his stone. *Christ is my life. Dying is my victory.*

My cousins Larry Downing, Ken Strain, and Bobby Hansch were the heroes of my childhood. Varsity basketball players in crewcuts and stocking caps, they were hustling ball-hawks who played the game with pride. Ken and Larry aren't here yet, but Bobby is. *Our Son. Robert L. Hansch,* killed at twenty-three in a logging accident near Neah Bay. When I was eight, Bobby was fifteen. One weekend my family paid a visit to the Hansch farm on Kroll Road. It had rained all week, and the pastures were ribboned by streams carrying the runoff. We spent the afternoon building dams, backing up water, and generally making a mess of my uncle's hayfield. Despite our best efforts, we couldn't stop the flow. It was like laboring over a sand castle you know can't stand against the surf: you do it simply to see if you can force Mother Nature to temporarily alter her course.

Years after his death, a classmate of Bobby's said in a letter to the local paper that when he died, the whole town grieved. I had been too busy with my own grief to notice. It was gray and rainy the day we brought him here. Hubbard's Funeral Home had set up a canvas awning for the family, but I wanted to stand in the rain. Somehow it made the pain more real. I remember wondering if the pasture on Kroll Road was flooded that day.

Bobby's dad is here—my uncle Otto. I was told his family was German, that he was born in Pollana in the Ukraine, but I have trouble accepting it. For me, Uncle Otto walked out of a story about Jim Bridger, a tale of mountain men who knew the land, knew how to survive. He could have played the lead in *The Old Man and the Sea* without benefit of script or direction.

Life in the Ukraine was harsh during the early part of the century. At times, the Hansches were forced to subsist on acorn soup. The family could not afford matches. Each winter morning, the children checked the neighbors' chimneys to see who had a fire, then went knocking in search of an ember that could be carried home in a clay dish. When smallpox struck their village, seven of the ten Hansch children died within eighteen days of each other.

When Otto's father died and his mother was shipped to Siberia, the only hope for rescue was his grandfather, August Hansch, who had escaped and made his way to America. August fired boilers for the Stillwater Logging Company in Vader, Washington, living on coffee and black bread and squirreling away nearly every dime he earned for two years until he'd saved enough to purchase tickets in steerage for his wife and grandchildren. The family crossed to freedom under cover of darkness at the border with Poland. Seven-year-old Otto was carried the final steps by a Ukrainian guard whom the Hansches had bribed.

After accompanying his grandmother, brother, and sister to the Northwest, where they were reunited with August Hansch, Otto eventually worked in the woods as a rigging man. In his spare time, he hiked every section in the Toutle River drainage, outfoxed game wardens with regularity, and maintained a still, which the revenuers searched for but never found. He lost a leg to gangrene after a botched operation following a logging accident in the early '50s, and while the wooden prosthesis slowed him down, it never stopped him from hunting, fishing, or running the farm. There was a unique rhythm and timbre to his voice, a rawness and depth that made me think of an old Indian warrior telling of battles from long ago. A bull elk lunges from the mountain backdrop that adorns his stone.

In the late 1940s, he took three of his children—Jim, Grace, and Bobby—camping at Yellowstone Park. Otto had a box of apricots with him, and someone suggested they be kept in the trunk of the car where the bears couldn't get them. No need to put them in the trunk, Otto insisted. He would sleep with those apricots between his feet; no bear was going to come into *his* tent and take *his* grub.

One morning, Otto climbed out of bed, left the kids asleep in the tent, and went to get water for coffee. On his way back, he saw a black bear pulling up the side of the tent with one paw and reaching inside with the other. Certain that the bear was after the children, Otto picked up several big rocks and ran screaming toward the campsite like Frost's "old stone savage armed." The bear must have figured this was a man to be avoided because it immediately began rambling for friendlier pastures. Only it didn't ramble fast enough. When Otto whacked it in the middle of the back with a rock, the bear decided a tree would be safer and scrambled into a towering lodgepole pine. According to the story, every time Otto shook his fist, the bear climbed to a higher limb.

If only the man who tried to steal Otto's car had known what that bear knew.

When he was in his seventies, Otto drove home from town in his Scout one afternoon and met a familiar car heading out of the driveway: his own

1966 Chevy Malibu. The drivers didn't know each other, and for a moment both sat and stared, unable to believe what they were seeing. Then the man in Otto's car realized he was in a world of trouble, trapped in a single-lane driveway by a very angry one-legged German. He bailed out of the car and attempted an escape up Kroll Road on foot. By this time, Otto had gotten to the house, cranked up his tractor, and, while Aunt Elsie called 911, begun his pursuit. Kroll Road is fenced with barbed wire on both sides. Instead of easing between the strands and fleeing into the trees beyond the pasture, the man panicked and stuck to the pavement. Uncle Otto closed in with malice in his heart. When local law enforcement arrived, the failed car thief was pinned between tractor and fence and very happy to see the police.

Some people might scoff at the notion that an unarmed seventy-year-old man could be dangerous. They never met Otto Hansch.

Jackie Roller is here now, but in the spring of 1949 he was student body president, an eighteen-year-old senior two months from graduation. On April 13 of that year, he was the single local victim of an earthquake, struck by a large chunk of cement that crumbled from a facade as he ran out the front doors of Castle Rock High School.

My grandmother, Amelia Roller Berndt, was his aunt. She was born in 1891 near Novograd Volynsk, Russia, fifty miles east of Rovno. The Rollers, and many of the others who settled in the Castle Rock area, were descendants of Germans who migrated east during the eighteenth-century reign of Catherine the Great. They were drawn to the Ukraine—known also as Volhynia—by assurances of good farmland, autonomy, and exemption from military service. At the time, Germany was governed by a collection of bickering despots and torn apart by the Seven Years' War, which had claimed 800,000 lives. The political disarray made Catherine's offer particularly appealing.

During the next century, nearly two million German settlers established hundreds of villages in Russia. German communities in Volhynia were notoriously tight-knit. They had their own schools to ensure the German language was not lost to assimilation, and the church functioned simultaneously as God's house and social club. Seventy-five percent were Evangelical Lutherans who viewed the Russian Orthodox Church as idolatrous; for them, the mere thought of conversion was abhorrent.

For nearly a century, the colonists eked out an existence, holding close to their culture with the reluctant blessing of the Russian government. However, the political climate began to shift in the last half of the nineteenth century. An aggressive "Russification" movement developed under Alexander III. Its goal was "the complete liberation of Russia from the foreign element." A series of decrees, passed between 1870 and 1900 and enthusiastically supported by Nicholas II, wiped away the privileges that had been granted by Catherine. Germans colonists were no longer allowed to own land or to declare immunity from military conscription. Under the new rules, Russian language instruction was required in every German school. These measures, combined with a variety of disasters, including epidemics of typhus and smallpox and several severe droughts, forced Germans living in Russia to look for escape in the New World.

Like the great majority of their neighbors, the Rollers were poor people: laborers and second-class citizens. Amelia Roller's mother died when Amelia was eight, and she was forced to take charge of the housework and care for her younger brothers, Emil and Ferdinand. An older brother, Frederich, came to America in 1907, and the other siblings soon followed, Amelia in 1909. They were fortunate to have gotten out when they did. Within a decade, the Bolshevik Revolution brought terror to the Ukraine. German colonists were singled out for harassment. Family members were separated, property confiscated, and loved ones sent to Siberia.

Amelia met and married Henry Berndt in Racine, Wisconsin, on July 31, 1909, and they came to the Castle Rock area in 1911, eventually settling on Tower Road. She endured eleven difficult pregnancies, all but one of the deliveries taking place at home. Grandma's sister-in-law, Bertha Janisch, served as midwife. Eight of Amelia's children are living as I write this: Elsie, Selma, Evelyn (my mother), Anna, Martha, Ed, Emma, and Walter. Those who did not survive have been laid side by side near their parents' graves: Baby Boy Berndt died at birth in 1914; Dorothy Marie lived six months before spinal meningitis took her life in 1933; and Grace died while giving birth to a daughter, also named Grace, in 1934.

While everyone remembers Grandma Berndt as "a nice little woman," she was the boss at home. She did the cooking and canning, supervised the vegetable garden, milked the cows twice a day, and made sure the chores got done. Since Grandpa was reluctant to discipline the children, that responsibility fell to Grandma as well. She would resort to a switch on occasion, but, more frequently, the tap of her foot and an icy stare were sufficient to keep her kids in line.

Amelia Berndt could not read or write English and was extremely apprehensive when it came time to take her citizenship test in the mid-1930s. Had the test not been an oral one, it would have been impossible for her. While Aunt Emma shampooed and set Grandma's hair in preparation for the evening classes at the high school, the two of them waded through the difficult business of American history and government. (*Who was the first president of the United States? What are the three branches of government?*) In 1936, Amelia Berndt earned her citizenship. The step was a symbolic one for a woman less comfortable with English than German, but the point was belonging and ownership and moving forward, and her statement reverberates like the chorus of an anthem in the story of our family.

In the spring of 1941, Emma was home from school with the flu, Grandpa was cutting wood behind the house, and Grandma was hoeing in the garden when the first stroke came. She stumbled into the living room, barely able to speak, and slumped onto the couch. Emma phoned town for Doc Emery, but his wife had the car and he could do nothing but give instructions. They held Grandma's head up and kept her warm, but another stroke soon followed, and two days later, Amelia Berndt made the trip less than a mile down Tower Road to this place, where she lies now with Grandpa.

When I was a boy, he never had much to say—or maybe he had no desire to share it with children. I wonder what he and Grandma talk of now.

My great-aunt, Bertha Janisch, rests here beside her husband, Frank. The headstone is marble. Their names are inscribed on opposite pages of an open book. Frank's life, however, could hardly be considered an open book. Once described as "an artist with a broad-ax" when he and my grandfather hewed bridge timbers for McCormick's Logging Company, Frank never revealed the secret of where in Europe he'd come from—not even to his children—nor did he divulge any stories of his past. But Bertha had a story.

Born Bertha Berndt in 1880 near Rovno, Russia, 100 miles northwest of Kiev, she was only a girl when her mother died from blood poisoning that started in a sore on her cheek. Bertha ran the household and raised her sisters and brothers—the youngest of whom was my grandfather—until her father found a second wife. Unfortunately, Bertha's stepmother died of tuberculosis within a year, and when August Berndt married a third time, it was to a woman who would drive his children away. At twelve, Bertha was sent to work for another family, far from Rovno. She was allowed to come home once a year, and then only to deliver her earnings. Her personal take for one year's labor was two new aprons. In 1906, Bertha's uncle used an illegal passport to bring her to America aboard a cattle ship. She lived with his family in Michigan for a time and worked in a cannery; even in her later years she could take the skin off an apple faster than you could say "Racine, Wisconsin," which is where her marriage to Frank was arranged. They had known each other for all of three days.

Bertha did not forget her little brother. She and Frank sent Henry Berndt the eighty-four dollars needed to bribe the appropriate officials and secure passage from Rotterdam to New York. He was twenty when he stepped off the *New Amsterdam* at Ellis Island late in the fall of 1907, unable to speak a word of English. He took the train to Racine, where he later met and married Amelia Roller after a one-month courtship. Word has it that Grandpa was engaged to another woman when he and Grandma were married, but the details remain murky. Despite the passage of nearly a century, the matter is not freely discussed in this family of tight-lipped Germans.

Along with Frank and Bertha, the newlyweds followed their dream to the timber country of the Northwest. The climate was moderate and jobs were readily available. The Janisches built their house on Tower Road, less than a mile from its intersection with Spirit Lake Highway, at the top of what the old-timers still refer to as Janisch Hill. Grandpa and Grandma settled a hundred yards away, initially on Tower Road and later, after the first house burned in 1919, just off the nearby McCormick Spur.

The home place is gone now, but when I passed today I could see where it once stood. The history handed down in unwritten tales flooded back like the smells from a grandmother's kitchen, and for a moment I imagined I had grown up there myself. It struck me that this was where my mother was conceived, where she was born, and where she grew up, milking cows in the morning before school, riding the hand-pumped speeder on the rail line that sliced across their farm, running barefoot through the stubble of the hayfield my grandfather cut with a hand scythe in the long evenings of summer.

Henry Berndt's stone is gray marble, laid flat, bordered by concrete, adorned with a cross and the word *Father.* What more need be said?

He was born in the village of Walinigen, Russia, in 1887. As a boy, he helped his father make barrels. Because the forests were the property of Tsar Nicholas, the first step for a barrel maker was to secure a permit and pay for the trees he needed. The trees were felled with handsaws and brought home behind a team of horses. Then the stumps were dug out and new trees were planted. Henry and his father cut staves to length, planed them narrow-wide-narrow, soaked them, shaped them, and pieced them together on a jig. Split willow strands hooked in notches secured the barrels, which were filled with water to swell the pieces and prevent leakage. They were then sold to local turpentine manufacturers.

My grandfather told stories of huge wolves that roamed the forests near Walinigen. Rural families like the Berndts kept their livestock in sheds attached to their houses. Since peasants were not allowed to own guns, pitchforks were their only defense. One winter a man on horseback was attacked by wolves. Neighbors later located his remains—all that was left was a foot inside a boot. When Frank and Bertha Janisch sent the eighty-four dollars for Henry's ticket to America, he did not hesitate.

In this country he worked as a powder monkey, carpenter, road builder, and logger. Only five-feet-four, he bucked old-growth fir—six, seven, eight feet through—into lengths with a handsaw, a daunting task best suited for men with patience. Sometimes he smoked his pipe or ate his lunch as he bucked, letting the ceaseless rhythm of his work carry him through the monotony of each cut and each day.

My grandfather was happy to be in this land of giant trees and elbow room and immediately considered himself an American. He learned English but could never shake his accent. He once remarked that the best cars were "the Page, the Packard, and the *Puick*," and in the evenings would say, "It is time to take my *bat*." While he sometimes bemoaned the fate of "us poor taxpayers," my grandfather thought himself as well off as any wealthy man. He was pleased to have three good meals each day, a roof over his head, and a warm bed. But, as with so many other immigrants, what truly contented Henry Berndt and eased the pain of being cast adrift was the belief that his children and grandchildren would have the chance to live better, more secure lives than he had lived. That promise made all the sacrifices worthwhile.

My grandfather once said that the most important thing a man possesses is his good name, and that it must never be damaged. I can imagine the shame and anger he felt during World War II when he was suspected of being a collaborator. The backdrop had been set during World War I when anti-German sentiment reached a fever pitch throughout the United States. In Pittsburgh, the music of Ludwig van Beethoven was banned. Boston Symphony conductor Carl Muck was arrested because his ethnicity somehow posed a threat to national security. Illinois coal miner Robert Prager was accused of spying, dragged from his home, forced to kiss the American flag, and then hung. German homes and businesses were vandalized, and government's only response was to require immigrants to report for fingerprinting.

An evangelist known as "Three-Fingered Jack" toured the Northwest, delivering fiery speeches aimed at purported German sympathizers and stirring up suspicion, hatred, and abuse. In 1918, the local Council of Defense requested that William Rhode, pastor of the Castle Rock Lutheran Church, no longer conduct services in German. It was a seemingly insignificant incident, but one that made it clear that citizenship papers were not enough to prove loyalty. The suspicion lay dormant after the armistice but resurfaced with heightened intensity at the onset of World War II. These people spoke the language that Adolph Hitler spoke on the newsreels. They ate strange foods, like borscht and pirogi, and named their children Anton and Rudolph. They were not to be trusted.

The *Cowlitz Historical Quarterly* has on record a complaint lodged against the German families on Tower Road in the mid-1940s for allegedly failing to abide by blackout rules. Although the matter was investigated, authorities found no evidence of violations.

By this time, my grandfather had retired and moved to town. He often dropped by the shoe shop of his old friend Fred Krieger for conversation— in German, of course. Word circulated of "spies" and "Nazi meetings," and one day the authorities showed up at my grandfather's house to question him. They found nothing. There was nothing to be found.

Maybe he wondered if the land of the free was as free as it claimed, or why a man was judged by his language and his last name instead of his character. But, from what I've learned of my grandfather, I'm sure he kept his wondering to himself.

By the summer of 1962, Henry Berndt had lived seventy-five years, the last twenty-one without Grandma. He was tired and troubled by a heart ailment, but at peace with himself and those he loved. He died on July 27, knowing that the journey he had made from half a world away would be the foundation for a family's future.

The early morning sun shines here, and in the late afternoon and evening, shade seeps across the hillside. Wind ruffles the grass and hushes in the treetops. In a stand of spindly firs just up the hill where my cousin and I once picked cones, crows mock my search for things intangible. In the distance, a woman's voice—"Get out of here! Go home!"—shoos away a neighbor's dog. Or does she speak to me?

A cigarette butt lies near the grave of Martin Maschke. It is easy to envision someone else who has come here as I have to remember and reflect. I kneel, press my cheek to the grass. It scratches and cushions like an old uncle's beard. I listen for voices and hear the story of myself.

That night at dinner I stare into the flame of the candle my wife has placed on the table. I see the wick and glow of a kerosene lamp, smell the cabbage and the bread. I see pictures of things I never witnessed: my grandmother humming her way to the barn with the milk buckets, the ever-present apron around her waist; my grandfather dancing with Anton Horst in the front room of the house on Tower Road, joking and snapping their suspenders while Yukon Driver pumped out a tune on his accordion.

I take pride and comfort in the magnificent history I share with these people who were truly strangers in a strange land. Yet my awareness of their strength and perseverance makes me doubt the ability of my generation to create a mythology that our grandchildren can store and wonder at. Theirs was a greatness born of fire. They left mothers and fathers, crossed oceans, lost children to disease, survived the Great Depression. Our legacy is to fight the daily commute, struggle with the mortgage, scramble to make payments on our toys. It is a pale comparison.

The Nez Perce live on the reservations at Lapwai and Colville. Each year they travel to the Wallowas at rodeo time, window dressing for a weekend in the place of Joseph and Five Wounds. Do they feel as empty and distanced as I feel as they attempt to make the richness of the past live again? We are merely playing dress-up in our fathers' clothes.

In my heart I know that we have lost the stuff of myth and are not destined to regain it. This day at the cemetery on Tower Road I remember those who have brought me to where I am. This song is for them.

The Glossy Prints

HEY WERE GOLDEN DAYS IN THE TIME BEFORE COLLEGE led me down the path to permanent employment, and my love for a woman brought daughters into my life. The corner of the planet where I spent my childhood was a comfortable, working-class neighborhood called Jim Town on the edge of Castle Rock. It was bounded on the west by the Burlington Northern railroad tracks and on the east by Interstate 5. Jim Town was a place that made sense, a place where I knew the people and the rules, where change and disruption were as distant as the stars, and every location worth putting on a map—the Big Maple, Bum's Trail, the Log Cabin, Pigeon Island—was part of my personal geography.

I don't often call up the memories, but they remain nestled inside. I have edited the hurt and the words spoken only to injure; jettisoned classroom embarrassments and the specter of adolescent acne; shrugged off quarrels with parents, fights with childhood friends, and insecurities that threatened to gnaw a hole in my chest. I am left with the best of the glossy prints. Like wonderful seashells, they defy valuation from any quarter but the heart. When the time is right, I press my ear close and listen to voices from a place that was mine.

Jim Town was like many other Northwest neighborhoods after World War II, peopled by young couples doing their best to garner a piece of the American Dream. Men went off each morning to jobs in the woods or at the mills in

Longview, while their wives hung laundry on backyard clotheslines, mediated their children's disputes, and served up meat and potatoes for the evening meal. For a young boy, it was the best of places. With more than fifty kids in the vicinity, there was always something to do and a ready assortment of companions to do it with. The cast included the Hanks girls, Georgie Vernon, Tom and Charlie Golden, the McCoys; older kids like Sam Ross, Wayne Lovingfoss, and the Helenbergs, who added a degree of excitement and danger; and my crew, which consisted of Mike Jokela, Jack Stagner, Skip Mezger, Eric Hansen, and Jim Ross. We engaged in combat with snowballs, chestnuts, squirt guns, and peashooters, danced our first dances to "Patches" and "Moon River" in Jim's resin-slick garage, fought with each other and for each other, and grew up together in a terrain free of drive-bys and drugs.

In the early days, Jim, Eric, and I were inseparable. Eric was a whippet, always first in a footrace, and the best athlete among us until a broken arm put a dent in his development from which he never fully recovered. Eric had two older brothers who taught him raunchy songs and racy vocabulary; he was the first in our group able to define words like *virgin* and *poontang*.

Jim was my best friend. A beefy redhead with freckles and a face like Oliver Hardy, he had an easy, rumbling laugh that held us together. His nose never stopped running, probably because he tromped through every puddle between home and school with the belligerence of a British infantryman at the Battle of New Orleans. Despite his size, he was agile, quick enough to snatch bees out of the air with his bare hands or snap his bat around on an opponent's fastball. We shared a passion for the New York Yankees and a love of competitive sports that consumed our weekends and summers. Each year on my birthday I could invite one person for a dinner of fried chicken, mashed potatoes, and red devil's food cake. Jim invariably topped the list.

One of the most memorable days of my life occurred when I was five. I couldn't tie my shoes yet and was still using a wooden box to struggle onto the seat of my Schwinn. That day I rode down the street to the brick house on the corner, where I tried and failed to execute a U-turn. I coasted to a stop, got off my bike, and was confronted with a double dilemma. In addition to facing the humbling prospect of walking my bike home, I noticed that the laces in one black Red Ball Jet had come undone. This day, however, there would be no humiliation. Not only did I manage to spin a decent knot, but I climbed onto the seat of my bike and pedaled for home, ebullient with the news of my twin triumphs.

Once I mastered the basics of bike riding, velocity became my sole concern. Eric and I loved to build speed on Woodard Avenue, which fronted our homes—standing on the pedals, leaning forward, driving our legs—then take the ninety-degree corner onto Balcer Street at flat-out maximum. We'd never ridden a roller coaster and had no experience with carnival rides. This was our first encounter with acceleration, torque, immovable objects, and other terms we couldn't define. We knew all we needed to know: we loved to go fast.

One summer afternoon when I was eight I had a close call on a trip down the hill to the town swimming pool. The road crossed the railroad tracks at the bottom of what we called the Big Hill. If you kept from braking and pedaled hard, crossing those rails could send you airborne. Legs barely keeping pace with the pedals as I flew toward the tracks, a speeder flashed in front of me an instant before I zipped through the intersection. I have a mental picture of the three men seated on the speeder: shirts grimed, faces drawn after the day's work, eyes wide with surprise, their mouths not quick enough to spit out words in response to the input from their optic nerves.

I began shaking as the grade leveled, and I slowed the bike to a crawl. I spent the afternoon swimming session pretending I hadn't brushed against death and hoping none of the men on the speeder knew my folks, who would certainly have blamed my carelessness for any accident, despite the failure of the crossing lights to function. From then on, when the guys chose that particular course for a thrill ride, I hung back. I hadn't learned all my lessons about speed, but I was in the process.

One day that same summer, Ron McBride showed up at our meeting place at the corner of Woodard and Balcer with a snazzy red bike he'd gotten for his birthday. It was a thing of beauty: chrome fenders, candy apple frame, racing handlebars with red rubber grips. Eric and I begged Ron to let us take it for a spin, and, after a good deal of well-justified hesitation, he relented. Eric went first, cruising down the block toward his house before he turned and headed back, gathering speed. When he reached us, he slammed on the brakes in a spatter of gravel at the end of Chet Hanks's driveway, locked the back wheel, and cut the handlebars hard left, firing a spray of rocks into the

Hanks's yard as he skidded to a stop. Ron tended to have a tremble in his voice under normal circumstances, but now he was misfiring like an ill-timed engine. "E-e-easy on the tires, Eric," he sputtered. "Yer gonna peel the r-rubber right off 'em."

We moved to the edge of the street as Jim Curry rolled past in the Standard Dairy milk truck and parked around the corner, across from my front door. Eric handed the bike over to me before Ron could gather himself for a protest. I traced the route Eric had taken, turning around at the end of the block, then building speed on the way back. The bike handled like a sports car, and I was flying when I whizzed past the guys and leaned into the corner. For a second, I thought I had it made. Then I realized that damn milk mobile was parked directly in the arc of my path. Jim Curry came out of the cab and down the steps of the truck with a rack of grade A homogenized just as I slammed into the side of the truck, splattering myself like a bug on a windshield precisely beneath the "n" in "Standard Dairy."

The next thing I remembered, Jim was standing over me and Eric was running to get my mom. My knees and elbows were numb, and I could feel a warm trickle of blood on my scalp. I was about to launch into some serious crying when a wail swept over me, tumbled down the street, and rolled toward the heavens. Ron had tipped his bike upright and was looking at it in horror. "Gaawwd, it's ruuuined!" he cried. "My dad's g-gonna kill me." The impact had crumpled the front fender and caved in the rim. When Ron lined the front tire up to roll the bike straight ahead, the handlebars faced hard left. Like a victimized rickshaw pilot, he picked up the front end and rolled the bike home on its back tire.

I was sore the next day, but my scrapes scabbed over, and I was back on the streets by the end of the week. Ron's dad repaired the bike in short order, and I occasionally saw Ron from our front window, tooling past the house like an old man on an afternoon cruise in his pampered Edsel. He got over his anger, and our friendship healed as quickly as my wounds, but I never bothered to ask if I could take the bike for another spin.

When I was nine, my fourth-grade class received a May visit from a fire inspector who left us with red plastic firefighter's hats and warnings about playing with matches. Jim Ross and I took the message seriously. Each afternoon we patrolled the neighborhood, plastic hats perched on our heads, pulling a wagon loaded with hatchets, gallon jugs of water, and several coils of garden hose, hoping against hope that we'd run across a fire and have a chance to do our duty. We'd been raised on the exploits of Superman and Sergeant Preston, so romantic notions of heroism perched like lapdogs on the front edges of our fantasy worlds. We were steely-eyed and ready for action.

Fortunately for us, my brother Dave and his buddy John Jokela were about to engage in a bit of juvenile delinquency in the lot that bordered our backyard. They had built a lean-to in a thicket of grass and head-high maple sprouts that had leafed out to provide cover and seclusion for their "fort." That spring afternoon was to mark their first and last attempt at roasting hot dogs in the wild. The day was dry, and it took only one match to ignite the paper and kindling they had gathered—and the surrounding grass as well. When they realized they couldn't stomp out the flames, they abandoned ship, their physical retreat an acknowledgment that the spankings they were sure to receive were a trade-off they had no choice but to accept.

Jim and I happened to be cruising by with our fire wagon when we saw smoke billowing from the maple thicket. We shouted with joy at having stumbled upon a disaster of such magnitude. Before Lil Helenberg, who lived across the street, could call my mother with the news, we had our hose hooked to the faucet on the side of my garage and were well on our way to extinguishing the fire, which was producing considerably more smoke than flames. Mom came running out of the house, first to learn if her youngest son had been injured, then to track him down and inflict injury upon him. She was so upset with Dave that she wasn't as appreciative of the heroic work Jim and I had performed as she might have been under different circumstances. But we were satisfied with ourselves. We strode around importantly, telling the neighbor kids to stay well back from the fire scene, secretly wishing the flames had provided a lengthier resistance.

We patrolled diligently for another week or so, but our only customers had gone out of business, leaving us no choice but to turn our attention elsewhere.

The Canyon is a narrow ravine off North Street, a block from the home where I grew up. Filled with gnarled maples and cable-thick evergreen vines, its steepness has discouraged development. When I visit now, the grassy hill adjoining it seems incapable of having sustained anything that might be called "a ride," but it was here we whooped and glided on our sleds when snow came. In good weather we played war games among the trees, aiming popguns and waving willow swords in a fantasy that would turn dark for some of us in less than a decade.

My right kneecap carries a scar from those Canyon days, when my escape from an ambush was ended by a barbed-wire fence that tore pant leg and flesh. And I harbor a distinct memory of a spanking with a wooden spoon my brother and I received when our play made us late for dinner. All the popguns in the world couldn't stand up to an angry mother wielding a wooden spoon.

The Canyon was also the place where Kerry Horn rode an ice cream cart into the land of neighborhood myth. Kerry was a year younger than the rest of our crew, but a member of our class as a result of having skipped a grade. We responded to his well-deserved promotion with the compassion and understanding of the average youth: we tormented him unmercifully. Kerry was a decent athlete and a nice enough kid, but he was gangly and naive, an adolescent Ichabod Crane with a knack for saying the wrong thing. When it was time to break up the afternoon play sessions and head home to watch "The Three Stooges," Kerry would say, "I must go home now." None of us were going to badmouth Larry, Moe, and Curly, but "I must go home" was sure to get a kid noticed in all the worst ways. Once, in response to this excessive display of good breeding, Jim and I designated Kerry our prisoner in a game of cowboys-and-victim, leaving him handcuffed for several hours to the basketball pole at my house, where his cries were stifled by Jim's well-used handkerchief.

When we were eight and Kerry was seven, his pride and joy was a shiny blue ice cream truck, a tricycle actually, with a cute little ice cream truck body and an annoying little ice cream truck bell that rang with every pump of the pedals. When Kerry got that thing going down a slight grade, it jangled like a runaway trolley car.

The Canyon's steepest pitch bordered the street where we rode our bikes. One summer day, Kerry came pumping down the pavement from his house, bell dinging madly, smiling like Reverend Ike in a sweet new Caddy. Our action was not premeditated. Maybe it was the bell. Maybe it was the immensity of the opportunity. Whatever the reason, we jumped off our bikes, ran alongside Kerry, and routed his little ice cream truck over the edge and down into the Canyon. Even when he'd disappeared through the nettles and blackberry briars, we could hear the bell dingdingdinging as Kerry rocketed to the bottom. It was an incident that soon became legend in Jim Town, and one in a series of pranks that Kerry somehow endured without mowing us down with his father's pistol.

Our parents measured the years with pencil marks on doorjambs, but our growth was better charted on the streets and in the sandlots and on the basketball court at Jim's house. Jim's brother Sam was six years older, so we didn't provide much competition for him until we reached middle school. During our sixth-grade year, Jim, Teddy Enderlein, and I squeaked out our first win over Sam in three-on-one. By the following year, Jim and I were beating Sam with regularity. Soon Jim was beating Sam, then I was beating Sam. When Jim began beating Sam using only his left hand, we lost interest and found new mountains to climb.

We played football, of course, a little croquet when summer dried the lawns, rode our bicycles with the reckless abandon of special teams players, and swam whenever we got the chance. But baseball was king. Those were the days of Mickey and Willie and Hammerin' Hank; Koufax, Drysdale, Podres, and the rest of the hated Dodgers; the Yankee wrecking crew of Whitey, Yogi, Maris, and Moose; Tony Kubek and Bobby Richardson and goggle-eyed reliever Ryan Duren, whose fastball was as likely to hit the backstop as the strike zone. Jim and I lived and died with the Bronx Bombers. We collected their cards, negotiating for them with the guile of horse traders until we gathered a complete set. Non-Yankees, excepting the Kalines and Musials and Spahns, were relegated to the spokes of our bicycles.

You couldn't go to the variety store and buy the entire league in those days. Collecting was an arduous process that required perseverance and one hell of a lot of Topps bubblegum. Back then, players changing teams was news, and the start of a season didn't require a guide the size of a phone book to know who was playing where.

Dizzy Dean and Pee Wee Reese commanded the "Game of the Week," and, fortunately, the network realized it was the *Yankee* "Game of the Week," for which Jim and I were very grateful. There were no ESPN games and no Monday night telecasts, only Diz and Pee Wee lazing away Saturday afternoons in shirtsleeves, with Diz popping cold ones from a six-pack and dripping sauce from a chili dog down the front of his shirt. Diz and his "old podna" Pee Wee, the first straightman in televised sports. Pee Wee supplied the who, what, where, and when, but it was Diz we were there for. He referred to line drives as "frozen ropes" and "country zingers," hooted at Yankee third-base coach Frankie Crosetti, sang the awfulest, wonderfulest rendition of "The Wabash Cannonball," and told stories that unerringly worked back around to feats he and his brother Paul had performed during their glory days with the Gas House Gang in St. Louis.

Initially, we played ball in my backyard, where our pear tree suffered permanently the effects of serving as first base. When we began to line shots through the garage windows, Dad suggested we find a new field of dreams. Shortly thereafter, he built a woodshed in left-center and we shifted our games to the vacant lot behind the McCoys' house at the south end of the street. Houses ringed the block, but no one had found a way to make use of the three acres that lay beyond the backyard fences, so we claimed it as our own. We played cross-out and cut the field down when numbers were short (anything hit right of the barn in dead center was an automatic out), spent hours looking for the one ball to which we were typically relegated, played until the seams split and the hide came off. On hot summer days we rested in the shade of hazel trees that formed our backstop, eating nuts and sweet Himalayan blackberries and plums from the neighbor's trees. We had everything we wanted: food, freedom, the game, and each other. It would never get better.

The spring of my tenth year brought us in a rush, armed with rakes and shovels and hand scythes to get the field ready. It was on that day Jim sliced off the tip of the little finger on his left hand. He wrapped it in his T-shirt and assured us he would be back as soon as he got a Band-Aid. What he got were twenty-six stitches and a protective metal cover. He missed nearly the entire Little League season, returning to pitch the last game, and losing when his shortstop threw to first instead of home as the winning run scored in the final inning. I hope he has forgiven me.

I see the guys at class reunions and bump into them at the grocery store once or twice a year. Now and then, we spend an evening together at the dog track or go out for Mexican food. But we are busy living our present lives, tending a new generation of families and stories, and have little need to travel back to a past that cannot be reinvented. In the old neighborhood, the legends have long been forgotten by everyone but the storytellers, and even they have trouble with the details.

We talk of those times on occasion, and about how the Saturday cries of kids playing catch or the breeze-borne scent of fresh-cut grass can pull the memories back in an instant. We have few regrets. We are content to have lived childhoods filled with magic and friendship and discovery in a neighborhood called Jim Town. It was our place, and it served us well.

The Felling Fields

OR MANY OF US, THE SECRETS OF THE PAST ARE THE DOMAIN OF SCIENTISTS scraping through digs in remote locales, excavating exotic bits and pieces of what was: the toe bones of a velociraptor that once inhabited Mesozoic Montana; shards of an urn from the Incan city of Machu Picchu, left for archaeologists to ponder; the leaf of a deciduous tree from the Cretaceous period pressed into the earth and preserved to tantalize paleontologists.

In the Northwest, the crumbling fiber of old-growth stumps clings tenuously to oddly hewn hieroglyphs that tell of the greatness and destruction of the forests that dominated this land in the early part of the century. Because they are held in wood, these carvings suffer the erosive effects of five decades of wind, rain, frost, and insects. Unlike the Sistine Chapel or the Mona Lisa, they cannot be cleaned or refurbished. In fact, few people would consider them worthy of preservation. Yet in their homely way, they are artifacts as true as any Sumerian goblet or Zimbabwe soapstone bowl.

Before power saws revolutionized the woods in the 1950s, timber falling was done with handsaws—misery whips or Swedish fiddles, they were called. Fallers working in pairs carried two saws, wedges, hammers, oil bottles, axes, and springboards as they made their way to the cutting each day. The springboards were made from two-by-six or two-by-eight fir and were approximately six feet long. Bolted to one tapered end of each board was a flat metal shoe with a sharp upturned edge. When the fallers picked a tree, they used narrow-bitted axes to chop holes for their boards three to four feet up each side. Springboard holes are about three inches high, ten inches wide, and four inches deep; they look something like an oversized mail slot, as if the tree were waiting for a delivery. The upturned metal shoe of the springboard was inserted into the hole. When the fallers climbed onto the boards, one on each side of the tree, their weight caused the hooked metal to bite into the wood, stabilizing the narrow platform they stood on as they worked. The boards could then be pivoted as much as forty-five degrees, allowing the men access to a good portion of the tree's circumference. As their name indicates, the boards had spring. When the faller rocked away from the tree, riding the momentum of his handsaw or ax, the board sprang down and then pushed up as the saw or ax whipped into the cut.

On steep terrain, springboards could provide fallers a level workplace above the salal and huckleberry brush that interfered with their labor. The boards also put the fallers above the butt swell at the base of the trunk; if the swell was particularly bad, the fallers went two springboards high—as much as six to seven feet off the ground—leaving a stump that might reach ten feet. In an era when only the choicest timber was harvested, those butt swells were left behind like crusts of bread on a child's plate.

When I crossed the driveway this summer to check the single springboard hole that remains on my five acres, I found that winter had taken its toll. Four clumps of huckleberry affixed between bark and wood continue to thrive and pry like predatory tentacles, transforming stump to bush. The top has crumbled away, but the bottom border of the slot remains, framed by moss and lichen. An offshoot huckleberry root runs through it like an exposed vein. When the wind picks up, the huckleberry sways, and with it the bark of the stump. Very soon, both bark and stump will weaken to the point where they cannot hold and will slough to the ground, where ants and termites will finally turn to earth the remains of a tree that once towered here like a muscular sentinel. It is part of the very cycle of death and decay that gave the tree life more than two centuries ago.

Not far beyond my house the pavement turns to gravel and becomes the 9312 line, a logging road that snakes through Weyerhaeuser country on its way toward Abernathy Ridge. A few years ago I went there to take pictures of springboard holes, but it takes longer to find them when I return this spring. My old place has been clear-cut and scarified, leaving stumps like charred headstones devoid of inscription. I am momentarily stunned by the realization that scarifying will wield a more abrupt and brutal hand than the elements in erasing the physical history of old-growth forests and old-time logging. There is something noble in succumbing to the effects of time, that age-old adversary we acknowledge and defer to in some fatalistic fashion. But to see the past erased by the scorched-earth policy of agribusiness is more difficult to accept.

Beyond the clear-cut, the road is lined on both sides with stands of slender firs. I leave the pickup in a turnout, step across the ditch and into the tree line, and begin my search for old-growth stumps. I find one, hollowed by rot, that measures seven feet in diameter. A delicate hemlock, five inches at the base, rises fifteen feet from the center of the stump, a potted plant feeding in the mulch the big tree has left. I can barely make out the horizontal cut left by the fallers in what remains of the bark. When I run my fingers across it, the delicate bark flakes, and I withdraw my hand like someone caught fondling precious museum pieces. Moments later, a pesky yellow jacket sends me on my way.

The ground is cushioned by moisture and the accumulated decay of needles, bark, cones, and limbs. Fern, salal, moss, heart-shaped three-leafed wood sorrel, and huckleberry flourish in the humus, but the going is easy. I move from stump to stump, discovering that as time passes cedars alone have the resilience to hold the marks, often only where the faller's ax bit deep enough to penetrate the bark to solid wood.

I guess the height of the trees in this stand to be 60 to 100 feet. Most are no more than two feet through at the butt. They would blush if they could. They are mocked by the stumps they stand beside and dwarfed by the red-brown remains of cull logs left to rot because of stain or a touch of decay.

Let your mind sweep away these pecker-pole replants, these tree-farm clones. Imagine a time when trees rose like rugged columns to touch the sky, rose like spirits from a mother that had nurtured them for half a millennium.

Conjure an image of the day the hole was chopped and the springboard inserted like a blunt scalpel into the side of a fir or cedar that soared 250 feet high.

The men who mount the boards wear no shirts; regardless of the weather, they work in black wool underwear, stagged-off jeans held up by suspenders, wool socks, and calk boots. They wear canvas rain hats or old dress Stetsons, brims pulled down to shed the water. They swing their axes in alternating syncopation, wide arcing strokes that carve a yawning mouth in one side of the tree to set the direction for its fall. Chips the size of playing cards pepper the air. When the face is cut, the fallers hook a toe under the back end of their boards and hop their platforms to an angle that gives them access to the backside of the tree. Each grabs an end of the falling saw, bends at knee and waist. (This fiddle requires two musicians to work the bow.) You sense the rippling of muscle and the explosive power that pistons the saw back and forth through the cut: *chew, chew, chew*—it speaks in the rise and fall of iambic pentameter. They hit a vein of sweet-scented pitch, amber and thick, but pause only to flick oil from their bottles on the metal to make the saw run smoother. Or perhaps they are men like Art Ferrier and Bill McCully, who forego the oil. "Piss on it," they say, as though the suggestion of assistance is an insult to their manhood. "We'll just pretend there ain't no pitch"—even as it hangs on their saw like honey on a butter knife.

As they pull the saw toward the point in the wood where it will meet the face chopped with the axes, they use thin wedges, hammered into the kerf left by the blade, to prevent binding and to coax the tree to fall in the right direction. Finally, the massive trunk shudders. A creak and a wrenching screech follow as the remaining wood tears away and the great tree begins its descent. They call out, "There she goes," bail off their boards, and scurry down precut trails to cover. There is a whistling like the acceleration of a mammoth turbine; limbs claw the air in a great rushing roar, louder, louder, then a final ground-shaking thunder that jars you from your feet to the hinge of your jaw.

For a moment silence returns.

The story is preserved in history books and old pictures, but the physical evidence of an era is disappearing, just as surely as the men of that era are slipping away. But for those interested in the history of this place and people, there is time still to view the ruins of an architecture that rivaled the columns of the Parthenon and the Temple of Diana at Ephesus. And time still to ponder the strange markings left by men who worked with the zeal of missionaries to bring it down.

Timber Country

F YOU SHOP AT THE RIGHT PLACES IN THE CASTLE ROCK AREA, you can buy novelty boxes of "Spotted Owl Helper." For a side dish you can purchase cans of "Cream of Spotted Owl Soup." Bumper stickers suggest we "Save a Logger. Eat an Owl." T-shirts boldly proclaim allegiance to "EARTH FIRST"—with a subtext noting "We'll log the other planets later." Black humor is a feeble weapon, but it is sometimes the only one available when your livelihood is threatened.

While it's easy to point fingers at the spotted owl, the demise of Northwest logging is a complicated issue. Environmental restrictions, automation in the mills, an erratic housing market, and a ban on export logs have all played their part in bringing hard times to an industry that has ruled the Far Corner for more than a century. Many loggers never saw it coming, and now they find it difficult to understand how things could have gone so wrong so fast. Much of their anger is directed at what they perceive as the hypocritical attitude of preservationists who purchase wood products in the form of building materials, newspapers, and napkins but oppose the cutting of trees.

As cries for regulation mount and employment spirals downward, timber communities have responded by building monuments and museums in celebration of a culture that faces continued decimation, a culture they believe should be valued at least as much as a seldom-seen bird. But despite efforts to stave off the inevitable, we in the Northwest are in the process of accepting that there will be no return to the glory days when one-log loads and old-growth timber weren't subjects confined to photographs and stories. Looking back can transport us to a time when the legends of landscape outstripped the story of any man. Remembering the past is certainly not a foolish endeavor, but attempting to live there is.

The story has always been that trees had value only as wood products, but now we are forced to consider whether forest in particular, and landscape in general, might have value in and of itself. For me, the issue is painful, the choices irreconcilable. I am caught between, tied by blood and history to the loggers, by heart and spirit to the land. It's neither popular nor comfortable to be an environmentalist in a place dominated by a jobs-at-any-cost philosophy sprouted from the seeds of desperation. Oppose that philosophy and you are labeled an extremist or an ecofreak, by those who don't refer to you as an asshole. And when the mortgage payments and grocery bills of family and friends are intertwined with the cutting of trees, taking sides is not an easy matter.

On the block where I grew up, timber translated into a living wage. Wes Jokela, Chet Hanks, George Vernon, and Max McCoy were timber fallers; Walt Mezger, a forester; Sonny Hicks, a shovel operator; Chuck Foster and Orlo Knight, paper makers for Longview Fibre. From 1942 to 1984, my dad was a gyppo trucker, an independent contractor scrambling to find work and pay the bills. A broken leg in a logging accident near Toledo, Oregon, ended his career as a rigging man in 1941 and left him with a steel plate he's carried in his leg ever since. When he was able to return to work, Dad and his brother Bob formed their own hauling outfit. Dad's first truck was a Jimmy he named Hustlin' Gal. After that came Federals, Whites, Macks, and Peterbilts and a working life seldom limited to eight-hour shifts. In the summer of 1960, he worked up the Lewis River on the east side of Mt. St. Helens where Muddy River runs out of the glacier at timberline. He got up at 1:30 in the morning so he could be on the landing by 4:30, made two trips a day to Portland if things went smoothly, and returned home around 7:00 P.M. I remember him snoring on a cot at twilight in the front yard while my brother, the neighbor kids, and I screamed our way through games of tag and hide-and-go-seek that he never even heard.

Weekends offered few opportunities for him to relax. There was maintenance and repair work to be done—packing and changing wheel bearings; relining brakes; repairing and rotating tires; replacing head gaskets—and when you drive for yourself, you'd damn well better know how to be your own mechanic because there's no money to hire it done. Winter brought wet weather, impassable logging roads, layoffs, and Christmases without much under the tree. Mom collected dimes in a Jim Beam bottle she kept in the cupboard above the refrigerator. When we camped or traveled to visit relatives in Tacoma, the dimes rode along as insurance against car trouble or emergencies. Things weren't easy, but we always had enough to eat and clothes that weren't an embarrassment at school, and when it came time for my brother and me to go to college, Dad's truck paid our way.

My parents placed a high value on education. After experiencing the effects of the Depression firsthand, they never tired of telling Dave and me that college was the way to avoid the economic pain they had endured and were enduring. My mother's family was fresh from the Old Country and spurred by my grandfather's focus on that most American of American dreams: owning a home. Dad's family was Midwest poor. My grandfather, Bill LeMonds, had tried his hand at tenant farming in Iowa and South Dakota during the 1920s and 1930s, but bugs ate the crops, wind blew away the topsoil, and the family was never able to put together enough cash for a place they could call their own. My father's formal education ended after eighth grade. Attending high school would have meant boarding in a town a hundred miles from home. This was unthinkable—he was needed to help with plowing, milking, and harvesting. In 1932, when Dad was twelve and the family lived not far from a store and post office called Wanamaker in the South Dakota Badlands, he worked on a neighboring farm for part of the summer. He and his partner milked twenty-two cows morning and night and spent the interim raking hay behind a team of horses for fifty cents a day plus meals. When the family came west to Castle Rock in 1936, Dad found work in the timber industry. It was a decent living, but one that was never separated by more than the thickness of the soles of a cheap pair of shoes from the reality of shutdowns and paychecks that failed to arrive on time. Like Mom, he saw a college diploma as the ticket out of financial instability and backbreaking physical labor.

For the most part, I believed my parents. From seventh grade on, my plan was to graduate from university with a degree in education. My brother, however, was a harder sell. When Dave was eight, he and the Foster boys from across the street waited each evening at the end of the block for Dad's Mack to rumble up the hill to Jim Town. Dad would stop the truck, grab his thermos and lunch box, climb out of the cab, and walk home while Dave and his buddies scrambled into the front seat. Dave would drive the rest of the way, and park like a pro in the driveway alongside the garage. The neighbors were apprehensive at first since he could barely see over the steering wheel, but there was never a hitch. I didn't express much interest in driving or in helping Dad with maintenance, but Dave was a good hand and a willing one. He made no secret of his dream of one day having a truck of his own, a plan welcomed like a bad case of gastritis by our parents. Years later he would come to his senses and attend Washington State University, but he never passed up an opportunity to push Dad's buttons. "I don't need college," he'd say. "I'm going to drive a truck." Statements of that sort were sure to set off fireworks in the house on Balcer Street.

The summer after my freshman year at Western Washington University, my educational commitment began to waver. I was selling shoes at a shoe store in Longview and with all my nineteen-year-old wisdom mentioned to Mom and Dad that I might put school on hold and enter the company's management trainee program. Nothing came of it, of course, but when I returned home for the summers after my sophomore and junior years, Dad was taking no chances. He had a plan to make certain I would be eager to head for college when the following October rolled around: he got me work as a rigging man with gyppo logging outfits. I tried to explain that I hadn't been serious about quitting school, but it was too late for retractions. I was about to discover exactly how glamorous working in the woods could be.

The summer of 1970, I set chokers for George Ells on a high-lead side west of Winlock. My first day on the job found me working in the bottom of a steep canyon with a soft-spoken man in his late forties named Bob. Halfway up the hill, almost directly above us, a stump the size of a motor home had uprooted and was now hung up in a clump of vine maples. I knew it was only a matter of time before it came loose and hurtled down the hill. I could see the headline in the next day's paper: *Choker Setter Crushed in First Day Accident.* Each turn that rooted up the ridge and brushed the stump had me poised to sprint down the log we were standing on and find cover. I was bent over, setting a choker, and Bob was standing behind me, when I heard the stump coming like a runaway boxcar. I made a 180-degree pivot that would have made Barry Sanders envious, tromped over Bob, and didn't look back until I was in the clear. The stump didn't get him, but it took a week or two for his wounds to heal. His wife was able to sew up the tears in his pants and hickory shirt, but the calk tracks I'd laid on him hung on for a while as evidence of my fear.

That first day typified the summer. I learned why choker setting is one of the most dangerous jobs in America and why few men last on the rigging until retirement. While I realized immediately that I wanted no part of high-lead logging, I proved my stupidity by voicing the opinion, in my father's presence, that setting chokers behind a cat might not be so bad. Flatter ground, I told myself. Fewer stumps-from-hell plummeting down hillsides. So, after my junior year, Dad got me a job with Ted Johnson. We logged right-of-way near Lake Merwin on the Lewis River Road from June through September. No matter how dry it got that summer, we never shut down for humidity. On the verge of heat exhaustion in the stifling afternoon sun, I could look down toward Merwin and see ski boats cutting wakes in the luscious blue water. By September I'd had my fill of horseflies, no-see-ums, and temperamental catskinners. I was also ready to admit that nothing was going to stand between me and a B.A. degree in education.

Now that they're long over, I don't regret those two summers. I learned what it means to really work for a living. It didn't qualify me for a workingman's Ph.D., but I earned a few credits and discovered what the degree required. I'd merely been playing, crossing days off a calendar that spanned three months, but for the men I worked with, the scene was real—and it was a lifelong proposition. They hauled themselves out of bed each day at 4:00 A.M. to face the possibility that a broken mainline or a widowmaker might kill or disable them. They crouched behind stumps when forty-eight-foot logs got loose from the chokers and tumbled down the hill end-over-end like twiddly sticks. They came home most nights sopping wet, their clothes steaming when the heaters in the pickups kicked in on the ride to town. They put themselves on the line for their families and were proud their physical efforts could translate into paychecks. They believed in a dream handed down to them by fathers and grandfathers whose cabled forearms and iron wills laid down the timber that built America: a dream that promised that for men who were responsible and strong and tough, there would always be work.

That dream has been rewritten by forces beyond their control, and many of them don't know where to turn in a world where grit and hard work no longer suffice. The scripted parts they play have been altered as well. A generation ago, they were labeled folk heroes, rainforest cowboys packing saws instead of six-shooters. Now they are called clear-cutters, land-rapers, foot soldiers for the timber companies.

During the 1960s, timber-related jobs accounted for nearly 15 percent of all employment in Washington. However, the outlook has changed dramatically for the Northwest in the last two decades. While timber harvests in Oregon and Washington remained stable between 1979 and 1989, employment fell nearly 20 percent—a net loss of 26,000 jobs—as a result of technological advances in the mills. Currently, the wood products industry in Washington employs 58,000 people who produce $2.2 billion in wages annually and generate an additional 213,000 service positions. However, experts predict that job losses due to continued modernization will persist, slicing 25 percent from the remaining workforce during the next twenty years. To make matters worse, the forest protection plan implemented by the Clinton administration in 1996 may wipe away an additional 12,000 timber jobs.

Things came to a head in 1990 when a double blow was delivered: the spotted owl was declared an endangered species and Congress voted to ban the export of nearly all timber cut on state and federal lands in Washington and Oregon. Timber sales plummeted, and there is no indication that they will bounce back. As a result, 134 mills closed, and 13,500 millworkers and 3,500 loggers were laid off. In Hoquiam, 600 jobs vanished when the ITT Rayonier–International Paper Company shut down the mill, sending the unemployment rate in Grays Harbor County past 20 percent. In 1993, Cowlitz County held its collective breath while Weyerhaeuser pondered whether to remodel the mill in Longview or drastically reduce operations here and shift emphasis to the South or to the East Coast. Their decision to maintain their local operation at its current level is about the only good economic news the area's wood products employees have heard of late.

Changes in the timber industry have hit gyppo operations and small mills particularly hard. Because the big companies own large tracts of land—Weyerhaeuser alone has 5.5 million acres—they have been able to maintain a relatively stable supply of timber. The small outfits, however, have depended heavily on state and federal timber sales, which are increasingly off-limits. Between 1960 and 1988, log exports increased twentyfold, from 210 million board feet to 4.2 billion board feet annually. During the 1980s, 4.5 billion board feet a year was logged on national forest land. That number has fallen by nearly 75 percent in less than a decade due to the crippling combination of environmental restrictions and the export ban. Seeing no other way to meet the nation's needs *and* respond to environmentalists' demands for the protection of spotted owl habitat, Congress invoked an export prohibition, severely limiting opportunities for small operators. Consequently, many longtime gyppos in southwest Washington—Olson Brothers, Joe Zumpstein, Ben Thomas, Jensen & Grove, Mayre Brothers—have gone broke or seen the handwriting on the wall and simply gotten out.

Mill closures and layoffs are nothing new to the Northwest. Washington and Oregon are dotted with dozens of towns where poor market prices or diminishing timber supplies forced operators to close. The Carlisle-Pennell Lumber Company in Onalaska once cut 300,000 board feet a day and employed several hundred people until its shutdown during the Depression brought the town's expansion to a dead stop. Ryderwood, McKenna, Vader, and so many other communities have followed the same route. The difference today is that the boom-and-bust cycle shows signs only of busting.

One of my cousins worked for Weyerhaeuser for a time before setting out on his own, eventually putting together a gyppo outfit, complete with shovel, cat, and tower. He spent a total of thirty years in the woods, but gave it up when hard times hit in 1991. He's fifty-five now and attending Lower Columbia College in Longview, finishing an associate's degree with his eye on a B.A. in business administration. Like the marbled murrelet and the native steelhead, he is an indicator species murmuring to us in ominous tones about what lies just beyond the horizon.

The Clinton administration promised funds to retrain workers displaced by reductions in federal timber sales, but for men who are forty-five and fifty years old and have known nothing but chain saws and chokers, starting over is a frightening concept. I once heard a politician predict that displaced loggers and millworkers would find jobs in the tourist industry evolving around the Mt. St. Helens National Volcanic Monument. I wonder what he had in mind. Will they hawk volcano trinkets in gift shops? Pump gas at the AM-PM? You may as well ask them to run the Tilt-a-Whirl or sell corn dogs at the carnival. These are proud people, unwilling to acknowledge that they are no longer needed. They are barely able to disguise the fear that is hidden just beneath their anger.

Neither wishing nor cursing will change the outcome, however. While logging will certainly continue in some form, there will be no going back to the big trees and unending sections of timber that lie in our memories like dreams of loved ones long since dead.

When the Forest Summit was held in Portland in April 1993, many small mills and logging outfits in Oregon and Washington shut down for the day to give their employees a chance to get their faces and their frustrations on the evening news. Environmentalists were out in force as well. The extremists included the Earth Firsters—possibly just back from an exhausting day of spiking trees—and a father and mother who had manufactured an inane sign held by their five-year-old son that proclaimed, "I want to be a fourth-generation logger."

My favorite banner was one that read, "The owl and the logger are both victims of greed and mismanagement." Those twelve words cut through the usual loggers-versus-environmentalists side-taking and describe precisely how we have arrived at our current state. It has been a cause-effect relationship with greed the cause and mismanagement the effect, and, while my heart goes out to those caught in the financial and emotional storm of the timber controversy, I have found I can no longer support the continued exchange of place for profit. For decades we closed our eyes and condoned the destruction of forests and streams, expecting the land to go on without blinking. While it will go on, and with a surprising degree of resiliency to boot, our claim that nothing has been significantly harmed or altered rings hollow.

Both sides seem to agree that we cut too much too fast. Even the old-time loggers are increasingly likely to express this opinion in interviews and feature articles that appear in Northwest newspapers. Early in the century, timber was harvested at a rate four times greater than could be sustained. Despite predictions from experts as early as 1938 that Northwest timber production would plummet by the late 1980s when low-elevation old growth was gone, cuts continued to exceed sustainable yield by 15 percent throughout the 1970s. Today's frantic public-relations attempts to salve us with heroic tales of massive replanting are akin to trumpeting the refilling of a lake after it has been drained. The question is not whether America will ever run out of trees, but whether it will allow forests to escape the sterility of tree farming and the madness of forty-year cutting cycles.

In Edwin Van Syckle's book *They Tried to Cut It All*, Fightin' Billy McCabe reflected on his life as a Grays Harbor logger in the first half of the century. "We did our damnedest," he said, "but we couldn't cut 'er out. She growed too fast." If he had hung on a little longer, Billy might have changed his mind. A survey of the landscape reveals that downsizing has not been limited to employment numbers. In less than a century, we have replaced our old-growth forests with the equivalent of Christmas tree farms. If we were speaking about the fashion industry, we might say that the Big and Tall shop has begun offering clothing saleable in Munchkin Land.

Last spring on Westside Highway, I followed a truck carrying fifty-eighty logs, some looking very much like large limbs. Thirty years ago, three-log loads were so common we didn't even remark when we saw them on the freeway. Today, the average load is often comparable to a fistful of uncooked linguine set on a Tonka toy. Each year, the rush for production means the timber cut is slightly smaller than the year before, increasingly knotty, and prone to warping. Each year, the timber industry grows more desperate, and the campaign to keep our heads buried comfortably in the sand grows more shrill. On the hill east of Castle Rock, a microwave relay tower rises above the third and fourth growth. If we can find a Stihl equipped with a metal-cutting blade, I suspect that one day we may include the tower in our harvest.

Our ability and willingness to hold ourselves responsible to the land are limited by a number of factors, most prominent being the fact that responsibility shrivels significantly when juxtaposed with our concerns for ourselves and our families. It is our innate sense of selfishness that allows us to survive and prods our brains to rationalize whatever action we take, morality be damned. Inevitably, we are able to talk ourselves into believing that what is personally profitable is equal to what is ethically acceptable. At the 1996 Western States Coalition Summit, a vehicle for the so-called Wise Use Movement, old-growth forests were referred to as "biological deserts" and support was voiced for 1995 salvage logging legislation, which made the incredible case that the presence of snags and windfalls is evidence that a forest is "unhealthy." Recent court decisions judged that the "dead and dying trees" slated for removal could also include ancient forest. Dead and dying? Technically, yes, if you pay no mind to the hundreds of species of mammals, reptiles, and fish that are dependent on such trees. Logging the remaining old growth will delay some layoffs. However, it is merely another in a long line of short-sighted temporary measures designed to win political favor while failing to address the issue of effective forest management.

The current political shift to the right has put the environment at significant risk. The Endangered Species Act is a prime target for those who believe in the flexing of economic muscle, regardless of costs that extend beyond profit margins and employment numbers. It's difficult to talk about managing an ecosystem without talking about more government, and these days, such talk is political suicide. Thus, at the same time the government released a study indicating that water quality nationwide is in jeopardy, Congressional Republicans introduced legislation that would ease water quality standards, reducing restrictions on industrial pollution and pesticide spraying and weakening requirements for communities whose sewage is treated and released into nearby streams. Conservatives call for increased local control, which ultimately means that when dollars are at stake, concerns about landscape can be overridden by farmers, logging companies, and developers who hold local economies in a stranglehold.

It is fashionable to claim that government regulation hobbles business, but consider whether business has demonstrated any willingness to regulate itself when stock performance and investor satisfaction are on the line. Which paper mills installed scrubbers to remove pollutants without the threat of legal action by the Environmental Protection Agency, simply because it was the right thing to do? Which logging companies voluntarily left wide swaths of trees along streams to protect spawning grounds, despite the fact that doing so would mean fewer dollars? Money has always spoken loudest.

In May 1994, the Cowlitz County Republican Party platform proposed that the environment be regulated only "to the extent that prevents degradation that would make it less useful to mankind." Thus, "wise use" has come to mean the efficient, unfettered exploitation of resources. This has been our history. Cut and run. Slash and burn. We exploit the environment as quickly and brutally as we are allowed to, operating in the manner that is most convenient and most profitable. While it is easy to blame the developers and faceless megacorporations, all of us have contributed to the problem. We sneak old tires into our burn piles and dump toxic wastes down the drain or over the bank behind the house. We fire up our wood stoves despite their effect on air quality and toss our recyclables into garbage cans headed for landfills because taking them to the bins at the grocery store is too much trouble. We offer excuses, but they are little more than shopworn attempts to rationalize our ecological immorality.

A second obstacle to our accountability is our unwillingness to relinquish the illusion of the Northwest as an unregulated haven for rugged individualists. We cannot acclimate ourselves to the fact that it has changed and that we must change if we are to preserve its integrity. Instead, we hold tight to our rough-hewn Western independence, hoping the land will right itself while we continue our business without interruption. "It will grow back" has been our adage, but a close look reveals that we have been kidding ourselves for decades, since long before environmentalists and the Endangered Species Act. As early as the 1930s Weyerhaeuser began to look for more efficient ways to reforest, a clear sign they realized growth was lagging well behind harvest.

After World War II, timber companies turned to national forests to fill the void that had resulted from overcutting on private lands. At this time, the Forest Service abandoned any pretense of protecting species and habitat, assuming the role of agent for the timber industry. Because its annual budget was directly tied to the amount of timber harvested on federal lands, the Forest Service went after every stick of old growth it could lay hands on. At the state level, a similar approach by the Department of Natural Resources led critics to refer to the DNR as "the Department of Nothing Remaining." Only recently—and only under a great deal of duress—have these agencies begun to take on a leadership role in managing state and federal forest lands in a manner that will sustain habitats and species.

Currently, 12 percent of Washington's land is set aside in parks and wilderness areas. When industry is not allowed to build or harvest in these places, people are angered or offended. A hue and cry arises because valuable tracts are being "taken out of production." Where the other 88 percent of Washington's land is concerned, we would prefer to be completely free to do as we wish, with no concern for consequences. It is the old question of sustaining both our standard of living and the quality of the place we call home, and it simply will not go away.

Despite our lamentable record, we have no choice but to play a role in the management of the land we inhabit. Nature has been subject to human influence for centuries, and that is not about to change. We can't be so naive as to dismiss the fact that timber is a resource. Finding the balance is the problem. Since we can't put a fence around our corner of the globe, we must demand that individuals and corporations take into account the connection between landscape and quality of life, even if this means increased regulation. With development exploding, we must manage. If we do not, erosion, pollution, and the eradication of wild things will occur by default. The question is whether we will acknowledge that species and landscape have value and agree to sacrifice a portion of our personal comfort and control in exchange for those things that have drawn and rooted us here.

A third dilemma affecting our environmental stewardship results from the brevity of the human life span. We are here for about seventy-five years, less than an eye blink in the history of the planet, and have trouble seeing beyond the narrow scope of our own individual existence. Typically, we wait until crisis is at hand before acting. Thus, when scientists warn of annihilation of the rain forests and impending crisis in the ozone layer, we scoff. We expect to see major changes overnight. When we don't, we use this "lack of evidence" to rationalize our argument that there are no problems. *Hell, if there was a real problem, the ice caps would be melting and half the towns on the coast would be underwater.* Perhaps things would be different if we lived as long as an old-growth cedar. During the course of a millennium, we might see the long-term effects of our destruction and be more willing to act.

Few baseline studies have been conducted to provide the kind of data scientists need to make informed and incisive environmental decisions, and the current political climate makes funding for such work unlikely. For example, a proposal to study kelp or cormorants would be destined for ridicule by politicians who see no connection between such expenditures and reelection. And yet we know so little about the world we inhabit.

Until operations were affected, the timber industry had virtually no interest in forest studies. In fact, timber companies invested 75 percent less money in research than other industries did. While most people are aware that erosion resulting from clear-cutting and road building has damaged stream life, far fewer know that it takes nearly ten years after clear-cutting for the roots of newly planted trees to develop sufficiently to hold the ground together. According to University of Washington hydrologist Bob Naiman, clear-cuts on steep terrain near the Hoh River in the Olympic Peninsula caused catastrophic mudslides in 1989 and 1990, ruining salmon habitat in the area. Naiman predicts that streams in this area will not recover for 150 years. Roads on private lands aside, the Forest System maintains a backwoods expressway totaling 343,000 miles, seven times the length of America's interstate highways. It is easy to see why erosion has been a problem for a riparian system that is the lifeline of the Northwest's landscape. A Weyerhaeuser Company study in southwest Washington revealed that 181 amphibians could be counted in only forty feet of a single stream! Until we acknowledge that there are no easy answers, that nature is exceptionally complex and requires extensive study and monitoring for us to make intelligent decisions, we will be left with the job of all the king's horses and all the king's men as we try to settle on a way to heal our world.

The cries of preservationists aside, logging must continue. America needs wood products, and beneath the hype, there is truth in the statement that trees are a renewable resource. A sustainable yield can eventually be produced without the problems of the past, but we must stop pretending that business as usual is an option.

We must begin by jettisoning the perverse notion that the national forests are the domain of agribusiness. Next, we must make it clear that a property title does not give an owner license to poison the land or harm the streams he or she shares with neighbors. Moving forward in this regard will require a better balancing of profit and place. It will mean testing to determine whether the poison sprayed to kill broadleaf also poisons animals that ingest the vegetation. It will mean preventing the fertilizer runoff and massive erosion that accompany clear-cutting from ruining the riparian system. It will mean changing practices that have resulted in the destruction near streams of shade trees necessary for maintaining a water temperature conducive to trout, steelhead, and salmon. And, ultimately, it will mean less clear-cutting and better planning to ensure a varied forest system capable of sustaining a wide range of species. In the past we ignored accountability because it was neither expedient nor profitable. Now we have come to a defining moment, one that requires us to consider what role we will play and what world we will leave to those who come after us.

The landscape of the Northwest has suffered extreme damage in the past fifty years. We have no choice but to reach a compromise, one that will inevitably demand extensive change and increasing financial pain. While the salmon and the owl and the marbled murrelet get most of the blame, they are merely harbingers of what lies ahead. Like a canary in a coal mine, these indicator species are more sensitive to poison than we are. When the canary dies, you don't shrug your shoulders and say that extinction is a natural process. You take it as a sign that the immediate environment is becoming unlivable.

A recent poll showed that 50 percent of Oregonians rate natural beauty, recreation, and environmental quality as the things they value most about their state. Yet if a public ballot were taken on whether to open additional national forest land to logging, I wonder if the voters would favor profit or preservation. We have yet to break free from the environmental manifest destiny we have practiced since we set foot on the continent: what can be controlled should be controlled; what can be used should be used.

Northwesterners despise immigrating Californians. We are afraid outsiders will change things, that in their sheer numbers they will extinguish the life of the place that holds our hearts. In Castle Rock, people shake their heads at out-of-staters surging through town on their way to view the blast zone around Mt. St. Helens. We understand that peering through the windows of a car or bus or motor home is not enough, that loving the land means interacting with it, whether that interaction be hunting, camping, fishing, or hiking. If simply seeing could suffice, we would be satisfied with snapshots and videos of our favorite places. Perhaps we could fool our minds, but our hearts would recognize the sacrilege.

Stuart Wasserman of the *San Francisco Chronicle* reminds us we live in a rain forest. "Take the forest away and all you are left with is rain and mud." Although the ancient trees are nearly gone, Washington remains one of the most heavily forested states in the nation, and that forest defines us more precisely than any other feature in this land. It harbors beneath it the vast untamed mystery that roots us here and the intangible secrets of who we are. It is our obligation to move beyond personal profiteering to living in balance with the land. If we are unable to do that, it will be our greatest failure in the ongoing battle to reconcile the power of our minds with the flickering promise of our morality.

Woodcutting

T HE LAST WEEK IN JUNE HAS BROUGHT DRY DAYS and moderate temperatures, ideal for cutting wood. I work across the driveway, taking down a good-sized maple whose rain-slick leaves had made the road nearly impassable through the wet days of winter. After my saw has grumbled through a knotty block from the butt of the tree, I use a splitting maul to section the rounds and then carry the pieces to my pickup. The bark of the wood feels rough through a pair of frayed White Ox gloves.

I am out of shape and my breath soon comes in gasps, but there is a primal satisfaction in cutting wood, a rightness and purpose in building a hedge against the future, squirreling away fuel to fend off the winter cold. The sweat is honest, the kind men once worked up as part of their daily labor, not the recreational variety elicited at step aerobics classes at the local health club.

While our heat pump is efficient, the wood stove in the basement provides warmth that envelops, the kind of medicine you need when November opens the door to the season of rain and chill. It's an order the air grates in the living room floor cannot fill.

My earliest memory of firewood is from the mid-1950s at my uncle Fred's when I was four or five. His post-and-beam woodshed had no walls to prevent the wind from gusting through and seasoning the wood. On hot summer days, when my cousins and I stepped into the shed and stood in the narrow passageway between the ricks, it was like walking into a root cellar. Moisture evaporating from the stacks hung in the air and closed around us like a cool, shadowy bubble. The overpowering aroma of fir flowed over us like the rich smell of fresh-baked bread.

Since my boyhood on Balcer Street in Castle Rock, woodcutting has been a summer ritual. Each year, my father bought a load of saw logs from whichever gyppo he was working for at the time and hauled them home on his last trip out on a Friday night. When he got to the house, he'd trip the bunk stakes on his Mack and roll the logs off in the backyard along the driveway. Some nights after work he cut a few blocks with the chain saw, and the next day my brother and I split the wood with maul and wedge and wheeled it to the woodshed. We stacked neatly, balanced rows with little wasted space. My mother was the champion of stacking neatly, and you did it the way she had taught or you started over.

In the Old World, my grandfather's family scoured the forests of the Ukraine near their tiny Russian village, gathering limbs for firewood because trees could be cut only with government permission. What must my grandfather have thought when he came to the Northwest in 1911? For those living in the greatest forest on the planet, wood for the stoves at home was merely another perq. Like the annual harvests of fish and venison, firewood was part of the package, a Northwest legacy in the days when we could afford to be careless. Cull logs were there for the taking, five and six feet in diameter, discarded because of stain or a bit of rot in the butt end. It was like picking up sapphires and rubies tossed aside in a land where diamonds served as currency.

In the late 1920s, my great-uncle John Roller once split nine cords of wood in a day, using a short-handled ten-pound maul he swung with one hand. A great grizzly bear of a man, nearly six-feet-four and well over 200 pounds, he worked for the Silver Lake Logging Company east of Castle Rock, busting chunks of fir into halves and quarters to feed the steam locomotives that carried timber to the great mills in Longview. Nine cords would total approximately 1,152 cubic feet and occupy a space twelve-by-twelve to a height of eight feet. Nine cords would carry me through a winter with wood to spare. Take into account that he was working with knot-free blocks of old-growth fir and it remains difficult to comprehend how such a task could be accomplished by a single man in an eight-hour day.

The fir logs my dad brought home were less imposing than those available to Uncle John. Two and a half to four feet in diameter, they were straight-grained and split like cedar. No one burned alder or maple in those days. It would have been considered a sign of deviant behavior. But by the time I had my own home in the late 1970s, fir was becoming increasingly difficult to find, and the trash wood of the 1960s emerged as our mainstay. We turned to foot-and-a-half and two-foot blocks of alder that split white and clean and held a fire all night. It was then I first became haunted by the smell of pitch and the image of fir; I have yet to shake their hold on me. The hardwoods burn just as well, but being denied the fir bothers me, much as I'm bothered by having to shop for razor clams at the grocery store when unexplained attacks by microbacteria deny me the chance to dig my own at Long Beach or Copalis.

Recently, a number of timber companies moved to increase their efficiency in response to a skyrocketing demand for pulp wood. Last summer, for the first time, I saw trucks pulling forty-foot trailers with short sidewalls loaded with landing remnants; everything but the limbs was being hauled to the mills, ingredients for batches of pulp stew that would eventually be served up as paper or fiberboard. Each year, the timber industry now takes out 15 million tons of pulp logs that previously would have been burned or left to rot.

Thus, I find myself having traveled nearly full circle, back to the woods near Walinigen, Russia, where my grandfather and his sisters gathered limbs. Ten years ago, the cousins who cut wood with me would have laughed at the load I brought home this week, and I would have joined them. It consisted of battered chunks of dusty alder and crooked maple, and cherry, four to eight inches in diameter, snagged with a pickaroon from the scarify piles in Weyerhaeuser country. Once an area has been logged, Weyerhaeuser brings in big D-8 cats to shove the brush and leftovers together in piles for burning. Of late, environmental restrictions have meant that the piles are often left as mulch. I don't take my saw when I go. Leaving it at home reduces the chance of being accused of cutting out of a stack of saleable logs, as some fools do. I cruise along, scanning the road for grouse and the sky for red-tailed hawks, stumbling across deer and the occasional band of elk, stopping to examine the landings and scarify piles in search of something I can hook with the pickaroon and load into the pickup. I throw in whatever I can manage without ruining my back, except cedar and cottonwood, which burn too fast to hold a fire through the night. I cling to this act of discrimination—my refusal to take just anything—as evidence that there is at least one level left to sink to before bottoming out.

Because wood is increasingly hard to come by, I add to my pile the larger fir limbs that have blown down on my five acres during winter and spring. Most are no more than three inches in diameter, hardly worth the trouble, but they would have to be gathered and burned in a brush fire if not saved for the stove. I also watch my alders carefully, taking out a few each year that show signs of decay. Once I've finished cutting the pile, I collect the remains for kindling—pieces of bark and scraps of wood the size of business envelopes that are stored in a thirty-gallon garbage can. One day each summer, I call my father to help with the extraction of blow-downs too large or too far from the driveway for me to move by myself. Along with his ingenuity, he brings rigging accumulated over the past fifty years for occasions such as this: straps, block-and-tackle, shackles, rope, chains, as well as his four-wheel-drive pickup. We run our own little logging operation that day, yarding trees to the driveway, where I can manage them myself.

This year, after cutting the wood into stove lengths, I was halfway through filling the woodshed before I realized I hadn't used the wedge a single time; there was nothing large enough to warrant it. Many pieces required no splitting at all. There was still the comforting *tha-whunk* of the maul in a few rounds that resisted division in one swing. For those I used the stroke learned while driving spikes on the section crew for Columbia & Cowlitz Railroad one summer: rolling my wrists and bringing the maul back in a tight arc, rising on my toes, pushing down and back with my hips as the maul begins its descent, snapping the wrists à la Henry Aaron and driving through with shoulders and back.

I take pride in living efficiently, and for that reason I don't resent having to scrounge for firewood. But I confess to more than a touch of regret at not hearing the ring of maul on wedge and wrestling those meaty, pie-shaped chunks that stacked so easily. This year, I split a length of barkless wood I did not recognize until the sweet scent of fir played like gardenia in my nostrils. It was then I realized how rarely I run across it.

The newspapers say Weyerhaeuser is considering locking the public out of the 5.5 million acres it owns. It would be a painful blow but hardly unwarranted. Already the process has begun. In the backcountry west of my house, the arterials are kept open, but gravel berms and wide trenches now block traffic to the spurs. Given free access to Weyerhaeuser property, people show their respect by stealing radios from the loading machines, siphoning diesel from the trucks, sawing firewood from marketable logs, and dumping appliances, mattresses, and every other type of human flotsam and jetsam, until even the great tracts of Weyerhaeuser are inundated and defaced.

Restricted access will limit woodcutting to special permit areas, something comparable to fishing at a pay pond. Soon, we will be reduced to harvesting only the limbs and blow-down in our yards, and this time there will be no sailing to new lands where logs the diameter of oak barrels were taken for granted as the domain of any man with a saw and a splitting maul.

Prescient Passing

AUTUMN EASES INTO THE NORTHWEST SO SOFTLY you may not notice summer is gone until you take stock of things. These are the blessed, damnable days that seduce out-of-staters with promises of wood smoke and eggshell skies. Sweatshirt evenings with the sun dissolving like a meltaway mint behind Abernathy Ridge and the crickets hanging on for one last refrain. To the east, Mt. St. Helens squats like a broken crown in a haze of dusky indigo.

Dawn brings heavy dew and a chill that pulls smoke from the chimneys of neighbors retired from the regimen of nine-to-five. Fog coiled in draws and caught on ridge tops frees itself, then settles like a congregation at the direction of a priest, filling the Cowlitz River Valley. From within the veil of clouds comes the eerie farewell honk of Canada geese wedging west to Willapa Bay or Long Beach, south to Bear Lake, Klamath Basin, or Humboldt Bay. Like the old-timers whose fires are the first of the season, the geese feel the change in their bones and respond without question to the rites of preparation, moved by a prescience of cycles and death and regeneration that many of us choose not to acknowledge, as though ignoring will somehow set us outside the loop that joins all things.

When I cross the bridge over the Cowlitz on my way to work each morning, the riverbanks are dotted with fishermen set on trout, silver salmon, and chinook. Boats hang in the current. Their occupants stand and cast into the fog for fish more spirit than flesh.

After dominating the stage through spring and summer, green is relegated to backdrop for earthen tones that light the hills until they glow as if a burner beneath them has been set on amber. Brassy leaves from birches in my yard scatter like coins on the driveway. By September, big leaf maples have reclaimed the showy title they held in April when their flowers came in neons that stretched the spectrum. Now on wings of death, leaves rise to a brazen beauty even spring could not impart. Like salmon headed single-mindedly for spawning grounds, they summon energy in a finale so grand that death must follow without delay.

In October, maples go yellow and haggard, leaves drying to crinkled rags that conspire with windless days to extend their display of vanity. Eventually they will drop and decay, gathering with them a year's worth of men and women on their way to the same destination without the grace that breeze and drift provide.

In late March and early April, wild cherry spent itself in a burst of white spring blossoms that heralded the season. In autumn, it is the first to disrobe, quietly and without advertisement. Alders lighten a shade and undress without fanfare, leaves thinning until one day only a skeleton of limbs remains, each mast left without a sail with which to snag the breeze. As the curtain surrenders its fabric, ridges are revealed beyond swaths of broadleaf stark and stiff as a dried floral arrangement.

Lacking the flare of maple, the leaves of dogwood, hazel, and cottonwood play a timid bass line in sporadic yellows. Vine maples fire sienna and orange from their tops, burning downward like wonderful Roman candles. In the clear-cut up the road from my house, they flicker in the wind like the campfires of an invading army.

Black-capped chickadees hang like fir cones in the alders, scavenging for seeds. A red-breasted sapsucker and his mate arrive daily to swiss-cheese the birch at the edge of my patio. They hammer holes in the trunk to draw a flow of sap, then feast on the insects the sticky fluid attracts. In alders and birches, caterpillars compete for leaves with the season, but their spinning is no match for the morning webs anchored on the mirror of my pickup, cast by spiders about the task of weaving symmetry from wisps thin as mist. I see art in designs that to them are as ordinary and pragmatic as knotting laces on a pair of shoes.

Finished with the apples and plums in my orchard, the deer who visited almost daily have faded into the hazel and huckleberry, taking the finches and chipping sparrows with them. They have begun their yearly rituals with hunters and rut and winter. Soon the rest of us will seek shelter as the weather closes in and darkness narrows the days.

One day in late October, frost comes with the morning, numbing the tips of my ears and reaching for the sensitive linings of my nostrils when I step outside to bring in wood for the stove. That afternoon, leaves drop in a flutter like crisp flakes of snow. An occasional gust sends them scrabbling onto the patio, where they crunch like cornflakes beneath my feet.

At dusk, clouds funnel in from the Pacific, lowering a misty gauze that fastens on needles and leaves, and the musical dripping begins. By November the storms will have come in earnest. Then, only the boughs of evergreens will remain to catch the raindrops that play the muted accompaniment to the long gray season that follows.

Rites of Autumn

I WAS TWELVE WHEN I KILLED MY FIRST DEER. Like me, she was just a yearling, only she wasn't armed with a Winchester .30-06 with a Leupold Pioneer four-power scope. She stood less than sixty yards away down a slight grade in a clear-cut, broadside, with her head swiveled toward our sound or scent in the fringe of jackfirs above her. Through the scope she seemed close as my fingertips, ears up like antennae, muscles along her back flicking and flexing.

As I snugged my cheek against the stock, fixing the crosshairs on her neck and applying gradual pressure to the trigger, a whisper of a question—*Is this fair?*—rose in my heart, but the rifle's booming report erased it, and we went to check the kill. The shot had torn through her neck, crumpling her like a rag. She lay with eyes open, head twisted at an impossible angle, blood darkening the fur around the wound. I was grateful her death had been instantaneous.

After Dad completed the gutting, his younger brother, my uncle Cliff, threw the deer across his back, and we walked up the hill to the pickup. I was supposed to be proud, and, despite my queasiness, I guess I was. I'd been taught that hunting was about more than homemade lunches, hot chocolate, rushing creeks, and October mornings with frost in the cutbanks. It was about bringing something home, and I had done that.

I don't recall ever making a conscious decision to stop hunting. I left for college at eighteen, and when I returned four years later I was married and had neither the time nor the interest. The uncles and cousins and friends who had camped with us in the big tents on the 320 line now hunted in groups of two and three. The chance for laughter and tall tales was diminished, and I never felt the desire to revisit the boyhood adventuring I had considered both a sport and a ritual.

While I like the taste of venison and elk and am happy to receive meat from friends and relatives, I have found I would rather watch wild things than kill them. Any edge I once had in the woods has dissipated, a victim of apathy and a lack of practice. When I see deer and elk I no longer look for ways to cut off their escape, search out a log or stump as a rest to steady my rifle, or calculate the trajectory of the bullet if the distance between myself and the animal is substantial. I find, instead, that I am awed by the grace of deer gliding across terrain that for me is an obstacle course, and by the tenacity and power of elk capable of walking through the tightest strands of barbed wire as though they were string.

During my high school years, I was blessed with a colorful band of hunting role models. For Uncle Otto, hunting was serious business. He was gruff and untamed and disdained waste like a Hemingway code-hero. Uncle Otto thought our elk camp was too plush with its cookstove and hay floor. There was a price to be paid when you hunted, and comfort was corruption. One elk season, he and his brother-in-law spent a night shivering in sleeping bags on a railroad grade near Devil's Creek. The next morning, Otto broke a candy bar in two and handed half to his bone-chilled partner. "Here's your breakfast, kid," Otto said. "Always remember, a hungry hound hunts the best."

Dad's older brother, Bob, didn't care much for deer season, but elk hunting brought him to the woods. For Uncle Bob, hunting wasn't a test of will or technique; it was an opportunity to see some country. The consummate road hunter, he idled through Weyerhaeuser country, gazing across canyons, stopping to converse with people he ran into, listening to his radio, and enjoying the heater. I believe my dad was always a little disappointed on those occasions I begged off on brush hunting and chose to ride with Uncle Bob. But what sixteen-year-old could be expected to say no to a chance to hear his stories while riding in a warm cab as Nancy Sinatra's "Sugar Town" played on the radio?

Dad's brother-in-law Bill never missed an elk season, but he was the most unlikely of outdoorsmen. Uncle Bill pitched his tents in depressions that filled with rainwater and was likely to forget even to buy a license and tag. For him, the season meant an escape from life in Tacoma. It was a week free from work and the city, a time to breathe clean air, drink some Old Grandad, and tell lies. One year, as Bill was packing a sopping tent into his pickup at season's end, he said, "Hell, next year I might even bring bullets." Unlike Otto, these uncles taught by example that enjoying yourself in the outdoors was the first order of business. If a dizzy elk wandered out in front of Bill or Bob, so be it. If not, well, there would always be next season.

My dad has hunted since he came to Washington from the Midwest in 1936. He doesn't get around as well these days, but each fall he hikes a trail that runs along a ridge across the road from his house. There he can watch a few openings and occasionally draw bead on a buck or bull. It is a rite, part of the great harvest that has accompanied life in the Northwest as he has known it. Six decades of steelhead, smelt, clams, mushrooms, and salmon there for the taking. I don't know that he has a choice in the matter; for my dad, giving up hunting would be a denial of belief and blessing in the land he has come to love.

Dad and I don't think the same way about the deer in our yards. When they make meals of my apple trees and rhododendrons, I grumble about the inconvenience, shout them away, or hurry them along with a rock. I anticipate that a percentage of what I grow will be theirs and accept the outcome as trade-off for their presence. Dad is more territorial. The deer are invaders come to raid his garden, and he pops them with his pellet gun or creases their ears with his .22-caliber rifle. He does not understand my attitude of welcome.

Despite my unwillingness to join them, I don't begrudge those who are hunters in the genuine sense. In fact, I find myself clearly connected to them. True sportsmen don't hunt to inflict suffering or to mock their quarry. They don't come to injure the land or to chop trophy racks from carcasses they leave to rot. They hunt because it is their way of paying homage to the hills and trees and all that they shelter.

Such hunters are worthy of respect. They talk of getting away and filling the freezer, but they are called to the woods by motives less tangible. They understand that to know and appreciate a place, you must walk ridges thick with ferns where stalks of devil's club serve as handholds, smell the brackish decay of unwanted logs, gasp at the sudden heart-stopping thud of a grouse's flight, see mist float from the draws and steam rise from the fresh droppings of deer and elk that have slid away like shadows. They have discovered that the land is a place to lose yourself and to find yourself again.

I suspect that what spurs them may run even deeper, that hunting proves they have not succumbed to the softness and decay that plague a society suffocating in technological comfort. Man once hunted for survival, not for sport, pitting his strength and savvy against that of the animal in a true test. Perhaps something primal calls to these hunters and they respond, not with trash strewn on roads or drunken target practice, but with the conviction that this is what is done.

This fall, the other hunters came to Growlers Gulch, rumbling up the hill in jacked-up four-wheel-drives and crippled pickups. They rarely waved when they passed me on my morning stroll, their faces bearing the serious-ness of businessmen at the airport or soldiers on patrol. Their legacy is left on the cat road that slices up the ridge where I walk: paper bags, cigarette butts, shell casings, beer and pop cans, a plastic container that once held "Coconut Crunch Munch 'Em Donut Holes." On a sandwich baggie a slug searches for crumbs; if only it could recycle the plastic as well. An evergreen blackberry vine has crept to the edge of the road, its progress not much slower than that of the slug. At the vine's tip hangs a perfect scalloped leaf, brilliant lacy vermilion against the blue-black gravel. I bend for a closer look and find the leaf has captured a Copenhagen wrapper. The leaf rests atop it like the paw of a cat on a befuddled shrew. In this case, it is the vine that is befuddled— *What do I do with this?* it may well be asking.

With these hunters, there is no respect and no compassion, only arro-gance and waste and stupidity.

Last spring I drove up Spirit Lake Highway, where I joined others in watching several elk herds in the volcanic blast zone west of Mt. St. Helens, each group numbering over 200. All deer and elk within an eight- to ten-mile radius of the peak were killed in the 1980 eruption. However, they have returned in large numbers to feed in a newly established refuge where they are protected. Far below the road, more than a mile from our viewpoint, they bedded on the mudflows along the Toutle River. While I was pleased to find that alder and foxglove and pearly everlasting had come back to animate the ashen landscape, the elk brought a renewal nothing else could match.

Several hunters gazed dreamily through their binoculars at massive bulls whose racks seemed to glow in the sunlight. I've heard some argue that the herds have grown too large in this protected habitat. They insist the elk will damage the fragile plant life and ultimately suffer starvation as a result of overgrazing. The animals must be thinned, they say—for their own good and the good of the land—and a number of hunters have volunteered to provide this service. Like old-growth timber blown down in a national park, we cannot abide what we perceive to be waste. We cannot permit the earth to do her work without our assistance. We have exterminated the predators that once kept the balance. Refusing to tolerate their competition, we have armed and appointed ourselves wildlife managers, keepers of the land of deer and elk. Somehow, the word *sportsman* does not suit this set of circumstances.

My hunting now is bound by neither season nor weapon, and there is no bag limit on the game I track. I am content to carry binoculars and bird books in hopes of identifying what I see and to share time and space with creatures I once tried to kill. I follow their trails beneath jackfirs and across hillsides like a voyeur seeking something he cannot provide for himself. I don't bring home any meat, but occasionally I snare something of their spirit, and that is sustenance enough for a heart that hunts the landscape's story.

Master Adapter

WHEN SHERRY AND I MOVED TO GROWLERS GULCH in the mid-1970s, I was surprised and thrilled to find that moonlit evenings carried the cries of coyotes one ridge away. It was and is invigorating, a sign that we live on the edge of wildness. Backed up against sections of open spaces rolling away to the sunset, the creatures the Navajos called God's dogs find room to run free and feed in the darkness. Their communal howling sets me to wondering: Is it part of some ritual tribute to the moon they worship, or the celebration of a kill, a dinner prayer sung to the night before bread is broken?

I saw my first coyote in 1956 when I was six years old. I had gone with my dad and Uncle Otto on a grouse-hunting trip. After traversing a patch-work of logging roads, Dad and Otto climbed the tower at Elk Rock Lookout near Mt. St. Helens and snapped pictures of the great stands of old-growth timber that stretched unbroken west down the Toutle River Valley. Afterwards, we covered more territory in Dad's Jeep—I don't recall whether Dad or Otto shot any grouse—before heading home. At dusk in a curve east of Kid Valley a coyote stood in the road. He couldn't outrun us, and the rock bluff on the upper side of the pavement was not an option for escape, so he took to the river, where Otto easily put him away with a blast from his shotgun. I remember being excited by the incident, as though I were witness to an adult version of the games the neighbor kids and I played with cap guns in the backyard. To a six-year-old, it was difficult to distinguish between coyotes and the

85

slavering storybook terror of wolves, and I was left with the impression that Uncle Otto had made the world a safer place.

Perhaps a sliver of that storybook fear hung with me when I began carrying a gun of my own. During elk season of my twelfth year, I waited behind a stump off the 306 line, watching the clearing across the canyon as Dad and Uncle Cliff worked their way up the draw below. With my binoculars I spotted a coyote, puffed and tawny, zigzagging down the opposite hill. When I heard him moving out of the creek bottom and realized he was heading precisely for me, the hair on the back of my neck stood on end and I went numb. In panic, I shot repeatedly at his rustling approach in the vine maples and salmonberry, emptying the chamber and fumbling to reload. I was shaking when Dad and Cliff found me, shamed by my fear and afraid to say I had broken a cardinal rule by firing blindly into the underbrush.

Years have passed and the fear has dissipated. I am better schooled now about the behavior of coyotes. I search for them on the ridge south of my home when snowfall publishes their tracks, but my dull senses are no match for their abilities. Avoiding me is merely a game, I'm sure, easy as teenagers ditching a little brother. I study their tracks, attempting to discern the rhyme and reason of their travels. One set of prints intersects another, urine is exchanged, the prints separate and move on. Like wolves, they are shy and haunting, content to melt silently into the landscape. When we see deer and elk as they wander into the yard or feed across a ridgetop, there is a sense of ownership and knowing that is missing with coyotes. These are not house pets held on leashes or ungulates posed in the lenses of our binoculars. Like us, coyotes are omnivores, hunters possessing intelligence and guile, driven by hunger, searching for a place to fit in a world of shrunken boundaries.

While Native Americans valued all animals, believing them to be embodied spirits that drew life from the same source as man, Coyote held a special place. Pacific Northwest Indians saw Coyote as creator, trickster, and fool and made him the stuff of myth. It was Coyote who made the Columbia River, who rescued the animal people from a great monster near Celilo Falls, who caught salmon to feed the elderly. In deference to his tenacity and adaptability, they believed Coyote would be the last animal on earth. Despite the efforts of man to erase him, there is evidence this prophecy may eventually come to pass.

As white pioneers moved west, taming the land with fences and farms, they sorted animals into two groups: labeled "good" were those we could eat or profit from; the "bad" were invariably predators that provided competition. An informal movement to eliminate these animals was instituted by ranchers who claimed their livestock were suffering severe depredation. The campaign was incredibly successful in wiping out bears, wolves, cougars, and eagles, pushing several species to the brink of extinction. The coyote, however, was more resilient. When the numbers of other predators were reduced, *Canis latrans* filled the vacuum at the head of the food chain, and efforts to eliminate the coyote were intensified.

Our tampering has produced unexpected results. In the Blue Mountains of Washington and Oregon, Forest Service officials took up the sword once wielded by hunters and ranchers, killing coyotes to boost the deer numbers. The mouse population exploded, eating vegetation the deer had fed on and ringing trees—gnawing the bark off seedlings at the base—resulting in a loss of wood fiber and a decline in deer populations.

In the 1930s, the federal government heeded the lobbying efforts of cattle and sheep ranchers, establishing an agency called Predator and Rodent Control—later, in a fit of dark humor, it would change its name to Wildlife Services—whose purpose was to eradicate "nongame animals." The agency is now known as Animal Damage Control (ADC). Over the years, ADC employees have shot coyotes from airplanes, caught them in leghold traps, poisoned carrion with Compound 1080 and strychnine, and drenched dens with gasoline before setting them afire. In a single year in the 1960s, 1,000 agency trappers reported the following kill total, which did not take into account animals whose carcasses were never recovered:

- 90,000 coyotes
- 21,000 lynx and bobcats
- 19,000 skunks
- 24,000 foxes
- 10,000 raccoons
- 7,000 badgers
- 850 bears
- 300 mountain lions
- an undetermined number of birds of prey

In 1988 alone, private citizens and state, local, and federal agencies killed more than 400,000 coyotes. Experts estimate that nearly 20 million have been exterminated since the turn of the century.

Ironically, a great deal of scientific data stands in direct opposition to the claims of ranchers and agencies such as ADC concerning the degree of harm inflicted by coyotes. In 1940, Adolph Murie completed a two-year study of coyote predation and published his findings in *Ecology of the Coyote in Yellowstone*, a book that refuted several misconceptions. While most people believed the opposite to be true, Murie concluded that predator populations are almost wholly dependent on the size of prey populations. He also found coyote predation of deer in Yellowstone to be dramatically overstated. He discovered that disease, age, deformity, automobiles, or hunters are typically the cause of death; most often, coyotes merely "clean up" the carrion. Even when adult animals are severely wounded or sick, coyotes prefer waiting until death has occurred before moving in. They are far more cautious than assertive and seem unwilling to risk a broken rib for a quick kill.

Since no credible research indicates that sheep and cattle in Western states are a major coyote food item—they feed primarily on mice, squirrels, snakes, birds, insects, yellow jacket larvae, fruit, and berries—scientists have concluded that livestock kills can be linked to a relatively small number of coyotes. However, with limited exceptions, programs to deal with such problems have been indiscriminate, resulting in the unnecessary deaths of "innocent" coyotes as well as other species inadvertently poisoned or caught in traps.

While some species have virtually disappeared as their habitats are altered or erased, the coyote has not only survived but prospered despite a campaign of organized eradication. Previously found primarily west of the Mississippi, coyotes have spread to the East Coast and the South in the last three decades as mountain lions, red wolves, lynx, and bobcats have systematically been eliminated.

There is evidence that coyotes are capable of learning and applying experience to enhance their chances for survival. In the Pryor Mountains on the Wyoming-Montana border, they have stopped eating carrion because so many sheep carcasses have been laced with strychnine and Compound 1080. Increasingly, they go after fresh meat—hardly what the sheep ranchers had intended with their poisoning. In addition, studies have shown that coyotes are wise enough to vacate areas under pressure from controllers. Thus, the programs in the West have surely contributed to the coyote flight to the East Coast and the South.

Coyotes have become new and improved in the Northeast. In contrast to Western coyotes, which weigh twenty to thirty pounds, their Northeastern cousins average nearly thirty-five pounds. Experts believe coyotes moving east met and bred with the last remaining wolves in the Great Lakes region, producing a stronger, more aggressive species. A study conducted by Gary Bundige and Rainer Bock in the central Adirondack Mountains of New York in the early 1990s revealed evidence of the changing habits of coyotes on the East Coast. Prior to the 1970s, coyotes were sparse in the Adirondacks. They hunted alone or in pairs. Deer made up approximately 40 percent of their winter diet. However, while deer numbers in the region have declined, coyote predation of whitetails has nearly doubled. These new coyotes—larger, more intelligent, and prone to hunt in packs—now rely on deer meat for nearly 80 percent of their winter food intake.

Starker Leopold, former zoology professor at the University of California at Berkeley and chairman of an Interior Department panel that investigated coyote control, noted that if biologists had set out to design a plan to increase coyote populations and make the species bigger, smarter, and more widely distributed, they would have been hard-pressed to surpass the accomplishments of those who worked so hard to eradicate *Canis latrans*.

During a trip across the Great Basin of southeastern Oregon, naturalist Terry Tempest Williams stopped to examine the remains of a coyote, its hide hung on a barbed-wire fence for all to see. "Another crucifixion in the West," she called it in her book *An Unspoken Hunger*. The message was clear: "Cows are sacred. Sheep, too." Over the years, predators have been killed without remorse or excuse. They have committed the sin of interfering with man's ability to profit, or they have taken a share of what man would kill for his table or trophy case. Unless we have seen the animal as useful to ourselves, we have refused to consider that it might have intrinsic value. A classic example of this narrow philosophy is a Montana law that outlaws "driving, rallying or harassing any of the game animals, game birds or fur-bearing animals." Despite the potential cruelty and lack of purpose, there is nothing to prevent snowmobilers and others from playing this twisted game with coyotes, wolves, or bears.

Our management of nature has been random at best. Since we cannot determine which animals are physically or mentally weakest, hunters may shoot those that are strongest, in the process removing some of the best stock from the gene pool. Nature is more efficient. While hunters and ranchers see coyotes hovering around a carcass and assume they have brought down a healthy animal, coyotes generally cull the weakest from the group. Those ungulates not smart enough or strong enough to survive are the ones taken, and the overall strain is strengthened. In fact, biologists believe deer populations in the Northeast are actually evolving in response to increased coyote pressure. Previously, natural selection was less of a factor. Now, only the fittest deer survive and reproduce.

One night in January, I was awakened by a frenzied coyote chorus in the canyon to the west. The wind swept their voices down the ridge, so that they seemed to be just beyond the line of alders at the edge of my property. As I peered into the night from a window in my daughter's room, I expected to see the glow of their eyes. On my walk the next day, I discovered the reason for their celebration: the remains of a deer lying just off a logging road like the wreckage of a ribbed sailing ship. Bits of viscous flesh clung to a skeleton in three pieces: rib cage; skull, neck, and part of the spine; and one foreleg. This winter I found the remnants of five deer within walking distance of my house. None of the five were located more than spitting distance from a passable road. In each case, the hindquarters were missing, a common tactic of poachers who dump the carcass wherever is convenient.

I try to look at things from the coyotes' perspective as I follow overgrown trails through jackfirs where they find sanctuary. From a hilltop near my house where I have located their sign, they can see the town of Castle Rock in the valley below, hear the endless rumble of freight rigs on Interstate 5 and the mournful call of trains, a wailing in which they may find comfort. Residents, sightseers, and hunters funnel up the road to the north. From the south and west come the bark of dogs and the whine of power saws and lawn mowers. Only in the bottoms of draws where springs feed creeks that rush and gurgle is there an escape from the sounds of human encroachment.

Surrounded by the presence of man, coyotes reply in the protection of night with the howling that is their stubborn cry of freedom. When daylight returns, they do what they must to survive, serving as scavengers, acting out the business of natural selection, remaining invisible in a place thrown out of balance. "We can try and kill all that is native," writes Terry Tempest Williams, "string it up by its hind legs for all to see, but spirit howls and wildness endures."

If we could pause to assess our motives in dealing with predators, resisting the urge to "manage" in a fashion better suited to the Keystone Kops than the complexities of the natural world, some sort of balance might eventually be struck. But unless humans are willing to coexist with predators, enduring the infringements of wolves and bobcats and cougars on those things we have claimed as our own, only Coyote may have the shrewdness and staying power to survive.

A legend handed down by the Native Americans of the Pacific Coast speaks of Coyote's confrontation with an *atatahlia,* an evil woman who lived near the mouth of the Columbia River. The old woman terrorized the people, each day tying one to a baby board (a backpack of sorts used to transport small children), which she sent drifting into the ocean with the command, "Go forever." When the board returned, nothing but bones remained. Coyote arrived to help the people and to test the strength of the *atatahlia.* Though he allowed himself to be tied to the board and sent into the fog and current, Coyote endured the journey and returned to exact vengeance on the old woman, whom he strapped to the baby board and sent to her death.

While we have done our best to force Coyote to "go forever," the species endures in spite of us. Until things change, we are left to rejoice at Coyote's tenacity. We must say our prayers for the others.

Risen from the Ashes

HEN MT. ST. HELENS ERUPTED on an electric-lemon morning in May 1980, I was watering my newly planted garden. Although the earthquake that jolted southwest Washington that day measured 5.1 on the Richter scale, I don't recall the ground shaking, only a flash of light above the knoll that concealed the mountain forty miles to the east. Within minutes, a towering column of ash and smoke frothed skyward. Area residents had experienced a number of false alarms—earthquakes and ashfall, spread over several months—but the size of the plume left no doubt that this was the real thing. I hustled back to the house, tuned in a local station on the AM radio, and listened with my wife and children to the stories of destruction. That summer, my garden would produce only ash.

Eruption activity had begun with earthquakes in late March, followed by a series of steam eruptions extending into early April. They were accompanied by the emergence of a crater, a sunken maw 1,000 feet long by 1,500 feet wide and nearly 800 feet deep, which marred the top of a cone whose symmetry had once been compared to that of Mt. Fuji. By late April, the steam eruptions had tapered off and things appeared calm, but the north side continued to swell, prompting authorities to evacuate cabin owners and residents of Spirit Lake. They could not, however, persuade eighty-four-year-old Harry Truman to leave his home. The crotchety Truman, owner and operator of the Mt. St. Helens Lodge, had lived nearly his entire life at the base of the mountain. As the campaign to convince him to flee heightened, he basked in the media attention—toasting reporters and responding to their questions with salty repartee, visiting schoolchildren who awarded him hero's status, entertaining a crew from the "Today" show with singing and piano playing—but he made it clear that he and his sixteen cats would not be budged. "I had some people ask me why the hell I stayed," said Truman. "That's my life—Spirit Lake and Mt. St. Helens—it's a part of me. That mountain and that lake is a part of Truman. And I'm a part of it."

Harry Truman's prophecy was soon to be realized literally as well as figuratively. At Wishbone Glacier, near the 8,000-foot level, the north side of the volcano had been growing at the rate of five to ten feet a day for several weeks. Geologists warned that an eruption was inevitable, their predictions leaning toward avalanches and streams of magma, but even the experts made it clear they were only guessing. People had seen news footage of lava eruptions at Kilauea and elsewhere; this type of destruction oozed forth at a rate that allowed time for comprehension and escape. It would be much more difficult to connect pictures, sequence, and understanding to the superheated gas and ash explosion St. Helens was set to send across the landscape and into our lives.

By the morning of May 18, the bulge on the north side was one-half-mile wide, more than a mile long, and protruded 300 feet. At 8:32 A.M., the earthquake shook loose the north-side bulge and 6.6 billion tons of rock plunged down the mountain at 150 miles per hour. It would be the largest landslide in recorded history. One leg of the avalanche roared into Spirit Lake, shoving water more than 700 feet up Mt. Margaret on the far side. Another branch surged across the Toutle River with enough force to top 1,100 foot Johnston Ridge and spilled into the valley beyond.

When the north side went, it was like popping the tab off a well-shaken can of soda. Superheated gas and molten rock found escape, exploding horizontally across the landscape with the force of 50 million tons of TNT in a death storm exceeding 800° Fahrenheit and reaching speeds of 670 miles per hour. Thousand-year-old trees were torn off at the base. Boulders the size of cars were flung like mortar rounds into the hills to the north. Old-growth stumps were ripped from the ground and tossed over ridges.

Mudflows followed the explosion as the intense heat melted glaciers in an instant. A torrent of water and volcanic debris rushed through the Toutle River Valley like a runaway load of cement poured down a narrow ditch, tearing out 27 bridges and 200 homes, carrying away logging equipment, suffocating fish, extending into the Cowlitz River and on to the Columbia where it closed the ship channel, trapping thirty-three seagoing vessels at ports in Vancouver and Portland. The water temperature in the Toutle rose from 50° to 90°, wiping away the entire fishery. Experts estimate that 70 million fish were lost.

The primary mudflow covered twenty-four square miles, raised the floor of the Toutle Valley more than 150 feet in the area near the volcano, and exceeded 650 feet at its deepest point. Castle and Coldwater Creeks were cut off by the debris avalanche and backed up into the canyons they drained, forming lakes. For months after the eruption, people feared the volcanic dams holding back the rising waters at Castle, Coldwater, and Spirit Lake would weaken and break, releasing a wall of water that would sweep down the valley, causing flooding all the way to Longview. Thus far, however, the debris dams have held.

As the mudflow and flooding extended west, an ash plume boiled out of the volcano like a muscular genie released from a bottle. Rising more than 60,000 feet, the cloud rode the wind east, coating eastern Washington, northern Idaho, and western Montana with one to six inches of fine volcanic residue. Yakima was blanketed with three inches of cementlike ash that refused to be swept or hosed away. Eventually, snowplows had to be called in to complete the cleanup. Throughout the Northwest, people wore hospital masks to protect their lungs. Schools canceled classes. Businesses closed. To the north and east, Interstates 5 and 90 billowed like dirt roads through farm country, visible from miles away as cars threw up clouds of dust that prompted the State Patrol to recommend driving speeds of no more than thirty miles per hour. Motorists resorted to wrapping rags and pantyhose around their air cleaners to protect their engines. One week after the blast, the winds shifted, and southwest Washington was greeted with an ash rain that brought down power lines and blotted out the sun like a Biblical prophecy come to fruition. President Carter flew in to declare the region a disaster area and provide promises of aid for people living under a siege mentality.

Two hundred thirty square miles of forest was now a moonscape. The whirlwind that accompanied the initial blast knocked down enough timber to build half a million homes. The mountain, which had previously measured 9,677 feet, was missing nearly 1,200 feet of its top. Fifty-seven people were dead, including tree planters, scientists, curiosity seekers out for a drive or an overnight camp, and one mulish eighty-four-year-old lodge owner. Yet the human toll could have been much higher. Because the blast occurred on a Sunday, logging crews were out of the woods. After the eruption, they returned to work sites previously declared safe, only to find the timber they had been logging was no longer standing. Had the eruption happened twenty-four hours later, at 8:32 on Monday morning, the death toll could easily have reached 500.

In May 1980, my brother-in-law's Weyerhaeuser crew was working eight miles north of the volcano near Fawn Lake. When they returned to their setting, they found the logs they had left stacked on the landing had been lifted by the blast and thrown into the canyon to the north. Their loading machine was halfway down the slope with its tracks torn off, partially buried in an ash dune. The tower lay in a heap, twisted like stripes on a barber's pole. Because Weyerhaeuser was anxious to log as much blow-down as possible before insects went to work and ruined what remained, the company got its crews back into the area that summer. Fallers and rigging men waded in knee-deep ash and lived with the constant fear of another eruption. Conditions were hard on workers and equipment, and a number of loggers left the woods for work elsewhere rather than face the prospect of eating ash and dealing with an active volcano on a daily basis.

Fortunately, there have been no major eruptions and no loss of life since the May 18 blast. Shortly thereafter, molten rock oozed onto the floor of the crater, forming a lava dome, as the mountain began to rebuild itself. A series of nineteen minor eruptions have raised the dome to its current height of 1,300 feet, but for now, the process has come to a halt. There has been no dome-building activity since October 1986.

People here underestimated the grief that accompanied the loss of a landscape we had reason to love. Nearly every person who lives in southwest Washington has a set of pictures, both physical and emotional, of Mt. St.

Helens and Spirit Lake. They are remembered fondly, like friends or lovers taken from us by a sudden tragedy. As a result, we have spent the years since the eruption engaged in some rebuilding of our own.

When I was a boy, our family camped at Spirit Lake during the summers. I remember the chill of the water, the sweet smell of fir mixed with wood smoke from the campfires, and the deep, indigo darkness once the lantern had been turned out. My dad fished for trout from a mass of logs floating in the west end of the lake, where he went after cutthroats with salmon eggs on a single hook and kept his catch in a wicker creel. If I promised to be careful, I was allowed to accompany him, stifling my fear as the logs bobbed in the water under our weight. Looming to the south was St. Helens, a picture postcard of a snow-capped cone. Dad shared stories of friends and relatives who had climbed the peak, and I dreamed that one day I would do the same.

After seeing the film footage on the evening news and reading innumerable accounts in newspapers, books, and magazines, those of us in the local area settled on the opinion that there was nothing left but a chancre, a shattered ceramic sculpture in a sterile desert of ash. There was talk that the landscape would never come back, that the ash was too deep to permit the development of significant plant life. Yet despite the passage of only a few years, the efforts of the land to heal itself have burst forth like flowers from a magician's wand, waiting like a promise for those willing to abandon their cars and do some observing.

While it will take many generations before a fully developed forest returns to the area around the volcano, the region's biological regeneration has been miraculous in light of the damage. After mudflows superheated Spirit Lake and raised its surface 200 feet, only microscopic bacteria remained. But as these bacteria, called anaerobes, fed on gases and metals, the water gradually cleared and sunlight penetrated the surface. Biologists have spotted fish in the lake and believe it is well on its way to returning to its preeruption status. Other lakes and streams in the area are recovering as well. Cascade frogs, rough-skinned newts, western toads, and northern salamanders survived in lake bottoms and beneath logs. They quickly recolonized posteruption waterways. Surviving brook trout and cutthroats swam to newly formed ponds and creeks or to devastated ones where they have taken hold. Perhaps most encouraging is the news that after initial problems caused by sediment, salmon and steelhead have begun to return from the sea to spawn in the Toutle and its tributaries.

Scientists first believed that life in the blast zone would creep inward from the undamaged areas surrounding the mountain. However, ongoing studies reveal that nature has proven far more vigorous and adaptable in filling the vacuum than they had presumed. Within three years of the eruption, 90 percent of the natural plant species had made an appearance in the devastated area. Another surprise came when scientists studying the recovery of species at St. Helens discovered that 70 percent of the Northwest's amphibians and 85 percent of the reptiles need downed trees to survive; this revelation led experts to recommend that all logging companies leave snags and chunks in areas they have cut.

The process of soil regeneration necessary to one day sustain old-growth timber is already well underway. Ground squirrels and northern pocket gophers, who survived the blast in their burrows, have speeded development by mixing rich buried soil with ash via their tunneling. Their droppings form a sticking, fertile base for wind-borne seeds.

Lupine has been another key contributor to the recovery. Like alder, it is able to survive in poor soil because it is one of the few plants capable of extracting essential nitrogen from the air and making it part of both its root system and the surrounding soil. Once lupine is established on a site, other plants will find enriched soil to root in.

After the eruption, insects immediately began working to break down millions of board feet of blown-down timber, processing it for topsoil. In addition to survivors in logs and beneath the ground, literally tons of insects have ridden the wind into the blast zone. Scientists estimate that 1,500 species of insects and 125 species of spiders now occupy the area around the volcano. As they die and decay, their bodies add valuable phosphorus to the soil. The insects have lured kestrels, brown creepers, northern flickers, mountain bluebirds, dark-eyed juncos, and other birds, which have seeded and fertilized with their droppings.

No large mammals survived the initial blast, but deer and elk have found enough vegetation for browsing and have returned in large numbers. They fertilize and spread seed via their feces and leave hoofprints that collect water and trap debris and seeds. Coyotes and cougars have come to hunt the developing prey populations.

It is an easy one-hour drive to the mountain up Spirit Lake Highway from Exit 49 on Interstate 5. The spectacle begins when the valley opens up at milepost 27 near Hoffstadt Bluff. Far below the road, the Toutle Valley has been raised and leveled by a mudflow now frozen in time and space. If you set your imagination free, you can easily see the floor of the valley moving again with the current. Deer feed along the roadside, and I have spotted coyotes and porcupines as they crossed. In the river bottom, elk herds feed and bed, safe from hunters. If the day is clear, the mountain will rise before you like an eroded molar, its west side fragile as a false front in a Hollywood ghost town.

Seven miles northwest of the volcano, the Coldwater Visitor Center—one of five major facilities now open along Washington Route 504—offers exhibits, refreshments, and a wealth of information presented in accessible fashion. From the observation deck, Coldwater Lake shimmers below in the sunlight, brushed by a northerly breeze. Beyond the ridge across the lake, mudflows emerge from the volcano like melted ice cream. Chunks of the mountain called hummocks, which made the journey downstream intact, now decorate the valley floor like nuts on a chocolate bar. The north fork of the Toutle River, fed by glaciers on the mountain, has cut steep canyon cliffs along its ashen banks as it serpentines through the broad valley floor, still seeking a permanent channel.

The real show, however, is not within doors. Elk Bench Trail 211-D, which starts at the visitor center, is too good for me to forego if the weather co-operates. Though exceptionally steep, the trail is spectacular in late spring and summer, a Matisse landscape featuring purple lupine and penstemon, deep mauve foxglove, lavender thistle, and tiger lily orange as an ocean sunset. Daisy, clover, pearly everlasting, dandelion, and Indian paintbrush accent the scene. The hillside is laced and bound by wild blackberry vines, and dotted with salal, nettle, Oregon grape, black cap, waxy salmonberry, horsetail, huckleberry, and tansy. I am accompanied down the trail by the feathered percussion of brown creepers and the buzzing of bees at work in the blooms.

At a bench where I stop to take in the panorama, a ground squirrel skitters by, transporting seedpods to a storage site below the trail. Its voice lends harmony to the chittering of birds until the sounds are indistinguishable. In the distance, the mouth of the crater holds a wisp of mist on the lip of the west rim. After plunging down from the visitor center, Elk Bench Trail 211-D connects with Lakes Trail 211 and meanders along Coldwater Lake, tying to Coldwater Trail 230 five miles in. Around nearly a dozen corners I am newly surprised by the sudden windsong of creeks, trickling, rippling, and slashing down rock runways to the lake. The streams can be traced in the river of alders, willows, and cottonwoods that ribbon up the ridge. The trees catch the wind in their leaves and sing it back.

After reaching the lake bank, the going is easy, the terrain relatively flat, requiring only an even stride broken occasionally by the need to tap dance on well-placed rocks across the streams that bisect the trail. The landscape is gravelly and sports a grand collection of Bunyanesque driftwood. A pathway has been sawn through overturned firs and cedars so huge that an accurate counting of rings would occupy an afternoon. Ants and termites scatter the trail with bright, fresh filings from the cut ends. The trail hugs the lake, which is clear and gravel-bottomed and drops off sharply. Water gurgles under logs and tentacled stumps that litter the shoreline. Newborn frogs small enough to be covered with a nickel hop frantically from beneath willows and seek refuge in the water.

The sign of elk is common, and I have stumbled upon them a number of times as they feed on the shelf between the edge of the lake and the base of Teton-like Minnie Peak. Hikers may hear the sharp bark of a cow elk that serves as sentinel, her call sending the herd 3,000 feet up the peak where they cross a ridgetop craggy as the vertebrae of a museum dinosaur.

At the end of the lake I have watched trout rise to feed on insects, heard the low drumming of blue grouse echo from the ravines, and seen the liftoff of merganser ducks in a tribute to the simple magic of black and white. The roar of Coldwater Creek picks up like a wind building far in the mountains, readying itself for a rush through the canyon. The trail skirts a deltalike wetland where the creek spills into the lake. Beyond that is white water, as the stream surges through a narrow gorge, polishing the rocks copper, with green beginning to streak through beneath the red stains of iron deposits. Above the gorge, a falls drops fifty feet, and not far past that is a log bridge across the creek where Lakes Trail 211 connects with Coldwater Trail 230 and others that can take you to Windy Ridge, the Mt. Margaret backcountry, Coldwater Peak, St. Helens Lake, Truman's Ridge, and on around the mountain. The fjordlike canyon narrows at this point, and the ridges press in with bulk and verticality. Here massive trees were tossed like darning needles, yanked out by the roots, or simply twisted in two. Snags bristle up the canyon like broken piling, and on every hillside trees lay like quills fired in some great porcupine war.

In the canyon, the ash is deeper, the vegetation sparse and less developed. East of the footbridge, the weathered root of a marvelous stump, its trunk ripped away during the eruption, clings like a starfish to a mound of rock. That it could have grown there, without benefit of soil or a pliable foothold, is remarkable in itself. But its tenacity in the face of an eruptive force that brought down brothers on better ground makes it doubly impressive.

A water ouzel searches for bugs where the current charges like a message from the mountain through a cut in the rocks. It is as though the earth is flexing, rolling up its sleeves and posing with knotted biceps, vigorous and confident in its greatness. Here on loaves of magma hunkered in the draws, I feel the land speak of eruptions and destruction and rebirth. I have climbed to the mountaintop on the south side, stood at the crater's edge, and peered into the throat of the volcano, but for me, this is ground zero. This is the place where the heart of the mountain resides in ancient arteries of stone exposed like cords of muscle in a sprinter's thighs.

Though neither my children nor I will live to see an ecosystem like the one that existed before the eruption, perhaps we have been blessed in a greater way. We are ticket holders granted admission to an ongoing show in which the earth remakes itself. I would never have thought it possible, but I have witnessed the creation of lakes, the decapitation of a mountain, and the raising of a valley floor. I tell myself that geography is not as distant as we might believe, that wonder alone might somehow melt the ages and transport us through this scene to the site of creation and re-creation.

Eventually, this dynamic landscape will give itself over to one dominated by alders and cottonwoods. The soil will continue to regenerate with each passing season, and, finally, the firs that have begun to reappear will rise above the broadleafs and the evergreen forest will resurrect itself as it has done so many times before. In the meantime, the mountain will go about its geological business. Scientists have discovered evidence of major eruptions in 1480, 1482, 1647, 1800, 1844, and 1855 in addition to the 1980 blast. There is no reason to believe there will not be others.

In 1982, Congress set aside 110,000 acres as the Mt. St. Helens National Volcanic Monument, specifically noting that the area must be left as is so that we may have the opportunity to see nature do her work. I have whispered my thanks a hundred times. Initially I came because I was curious. I wanted to stand where wind and fire had scoured the earth, to conjure images of that cataclysmic moment. It took only one trip for me to move beyond such cinematic imagining. I come now to rub against the mountain and examine the sublime workings of the planet. In a world of human failings, I never cease to be awed by nature's seamless intertwining of the power of destruction and the grace and beauty of healing. Fact and faith, it is both my science and my religion.

The Kid
in Right Field

HEN I SAW HIS PICTURE IN THE NEWSPAPER, I didn't realize it was Don McCoy. What was easier to determine was that the person shown in the photo was dying and had very little time remaining. Only after I read the caption and studied the face more closely did I recognize the remnants of a friend from the Jim Town neighborhood of long ago.

The photograph could have served as an advertisement for AIDS prevention, or as a call for compassion. Don sat in a wheelchair. The fabric of his hospital gown, the wild strands of hair, and the ashen fleece of his beard conspired to drain him of color. The photo was black and white but dominated by gray, and I was left with the feeling that Kodachrome would have changed nothing. The life and color had been sucked away by disease, and Don McCoy was little more than a husk of his former self, forty-two years old and staring death directly in the face.

Beneath his shroud, clavicles and elbows and shoulder joints poked at the material like limbs on a leafless tree. His eyes were sunk deep, rimmed in darkness beneath wire-framed glasses. His head tilted forward as though his chin was drawn by a string toward the middle of his chest. A cigarette hung from the fingers of his right hand. His expression acknowledged his acceptance: his mouth a slash, barely open, pulled up at one corner, as if to ask a question for which there was no answer. In the article he talked of fighting, of getting back to things he'd been forced to leave undone, but his eyes and the slackness of his jaw said otherwise.

I hadn't seen Don for nearly thirty years. He'd lived just a few minutes down the freeway from me for much of his adult life, so we'd probably passed each other in the grocery store or stood in the same line at Target. But if our paths crossed, I never recognized him. I carry no mental pictures of the person in the photograph, nor of the healthy man he must have been in his twenties or thirties. In my mind's eye, I see a gangly kid with dark, wiry hair who lived down the block in the days of my boyhood.

The McCoys lived at the south end of Woodard Avenue, half a minute from my house. They were very much like the rest of us: a working class family with bikes in the driveway and unpaid bills on the kitchen counter. Don's father, Max McCoy, was a climber during his early days in the woods. Later, he ran yarder for Weyerhaeuser and a number of local gyppos until he retired in 1977. On July and August evenings, he sat on his front porch in a sleeveless white T-shirt, reading the paper and letting the breeze carry away the smell of diesel and the grinding day-long roar of machinery. His wife, Lucille, was a big-boned woman with curly hennaed hair. She wore a brace and walked with a noticeable limp, leftovers from a childhood bout with polio. Despite the withered leg, the set of Lucille's jaw made you believe she was strong enough to gather all five of her children on her back and walk right through a wall. She nearly lost her oldest boy, Mike, in Vietnam. He was wounded in a firefight on the Bongson Plains in January 1968. Despite its napalm horror and the newsreel nightmares it triggered, war consisted of images, a landscape in which a mother could place her son, then cross her fingers and say the prayers that would bring him home safely. There was, however, no way Lucille could have foreseen the grief her third son's personal biology would bring him. No way to imagine a disease like this one, lying in wait on calendars that had not yet been printed.

When he was a young boy, Don had trouble pronouncing the letter *r*. We liked to ask him his name just to hear him say "Donald Boose (Bruce) McCoy." My mental portraits of Don boil down to a central image of him at nine or ten, hands jammed in the pockets of his Levi's, shoulders back in the posture of a man engaged in barbershop conversation, feet angled out, ducklike. His head bobbed in manic fashion, and behind the black-framed glasses his eyes were wide, brows arched as though awaiting a response to a riddle he'd told you. He wore short-sleeved madras shirts and black dress shoes, which contributed to the impression that he was a middle-aged man forced to play at the life of a boy.

In our neighborhood, sports were every kid's obsession. We slid and tackled and fouled with the verve of young cats, threw enough elbows and brushback pitches to terrify our mothers, and argued like a gaggle of Billy Martins over every close call. Everybody played and everybody was serious. Except Don. He was shoved into the mix by expectations that told him this was what young boys did; there were no other options.

We played baseball in a vacant field behind the McCoys' house, and Don usually joined in. Maybe at that stage he still retained the notion that he could be a part of things. When it was his turn to hit, Don kept the barrel of the bat on his shoulder, reluctant to take a cut. He never bent his knees, just leaned over the plate from the waist with his elbows out and watched the pitches sail by. When we ridiculed him for taking pitch after pitch, he responded with vaudevillian swings, flailing the air like a man trying to fend off bees with a toilet plunger. It was his way of dealing with a lack of athletic ability and the daily summer humiliation of being chosen last in any game we played.

Don's dad was the coach of the Roller Brothers, a Little League team that featured six kids from our Jim Town neighborhood, including Don's older brother Matt, who played third base for us. Like it or not, when he was nine, Don became a member of the team. His favorite moments were in the dugout during the early innings. He built roads and walls and villages in the sand floor, while the rest of us whooped and chattered in response to base hits and overthrows. For Don, the games were merely background noise.

It was the late innings he hated, the part of the game when Little League rules required that every kid get a shot, even those who didn't want one. He invariably played right field, the land of exile where the worst player is stuck in hopes that nothing will come his way. His fielding stance could vary radically, from ramrod straight as he stared toward activity at the concession stand, to an exaggerated hands-on-knees, mitt-pounding frenzy that came across as a mock attempt to involve himself in things he didn't care about. When a ball was hit his way, he disregarded suggestions to "get in front of it." Instead, he'd run alongside the ball until it began to slow, then pounce on it and throw back to the infield in that stiff, elbow-wrist motion of the nonpractitioner.

It was at the plate where things turned ugly, particularly if the game was on the line. We'd yell encouragement from the dugout, hoping for a miracle, but he had to know what we were actually saying was: "Why does it have to be Don? He's gonna fan for sure." He took things more seriously during Little League games than in the pickup contests played in the field behind his house, but the results were the same whether he was trying to make contact or entertain us.

I was several years older than Don, so we lost touch when high school turned my attention to girls and cars. By then, the old gang no longer gathered behind the McCoy house to play ball. Our friendship wasn't strong enough to bridge the gap, and our paths never brought us together again.

I didn't know Don was gay until I read an article in the local paper several years ago that told of the death of his companion, Rex Hendrickson, after a battle with AIDS. In an interview, Don talked of the heartbreak of losing Rex, but his anger and sorrow were tempered by the knowledge that his own illness was on the edge of eruption.

Seeing Don's ghostly picture last week, I was struck by the distance between his emaciated appearance and the plans he shared with the reporter to return to his gardening and to somehow call forth enough strength for a white-water rafting trip in central Oregon. Something in his words was hopeful, almost as though wishing alone could heal him and restore the life he once had. But ultimately, his wishes were for simple things, doable things: MTV, a burger and fries from Jack-in-the-Box, a chance to sit in his recliner and enjoy a cigarette.

Skin flakes from his cheeks. His lips are parched. His retinas are bleeding. He suffers from tuberculosis and pneumonia. In a single month he lost twenty pounds. He has moved into his parents' house, the same house in Jim Town where he grew up. Max and Lucille will care for him and love him and make his death as easy as they can make it.

I've never thought of Don as wicked or disgusting, never considered him an abomination. Despite the consequences, he is no more able to deny his sexuality than he was able to transform himself into an athlete. As he dies in his parents' home in the old neighborhood, he's just Donald "Boose" McCoy, the kid from down the block who couldn't hit a baseball.

Scripture for the Land

And God said, Let us make man in our image, after our likeness: and let them have dominion over the fish of the sea, and over the fowl of the air, and over cattle, and over all the earth, and over every creeping thing that creepeth upon the earth.

—Genesis 1:26

THIS PASSAGE, TWENTY-SIX VERSES INTO THE CREATION STORY, has proven to be the most destructive sentence ever written. For in it, man has found an unassailable rationale for the eradication of land and life in the name of personal profiteering. No discussion. No compromise. Nothing less than sovereign control by human lords and masters over every facet of the earth.

Where did it all go wrong? How did these forty-nine words find their way into a sacred book where they would serve as edict for greed and ruin? We've been told the Bible is the unerring replication of the word of God, but I am inclined to believe a mortal inserted that verse. It is easy to imagine that this man was not so different from us. He looked to the future and, seeing what might trouble a conscience, sought to head it off by contriving a justification that boasted God's own seal of approval. For a race set on plunder, these words have provided both divine sanction for self-aggrandizement and spiritual anesthetic for sins against the Earth Mother.

For those who insist God penned Genesis 1:26, it is reasonable to assume that if he gave us dominion he expected we would exercise some reason. That, charged with the maintenance of what he had created, we would treat it as a sacred work by an infinite master. We would see that our dominion over the land was comparable to God's dominion over us: it would involve compassion, sacrifice, stewardship, and love.

111

In any case, we have failed miserably. We have come to see ourselves, and God as well, not as a part of the natural world, but apart from it.

Ego and self-interest have closed our minds to the soundness of the logic offered by Ralph Waldo Emerson and his fellow transcendentalists, whose belief in the perfectability of man dominated American writing and thinking in the middle part of the nineteenth century. Admitting, as they did, that all things are infused with the Creator's greatness would force us to acknowledge that the natural world is as important as we are and require that we treat it equitably. This is an accountability we refuse to accept. That we have come to consider ourselves a higher power than the planet and the God who fashioned it has been our gravest, most reprehensible sin. Other cries of "humanism" and finger-pointing at man's misplaced worship of himself pale in comparison with our relegation of the earth to the status of a pantry, a cupboard filled with goods we believe ourselves obliged to use until empty, with no consideration of repayment.

Emerson and his protégé, Henry David Thoreau, were spiritual men, but not of the fashion seen on programs beamed in by satellite today featuring the doughy, silver-tongued whiners who serve as God's accountants. Collecting and disbursing tithes as they see fit, they would have us believe that religion and economics are wholly suitable bedfellows. Emerson and Thoreau, on the other hand, did not find it necessary to twist Genesis 1:26 into a justification of exploitation as God's will. They believed man had been granted heart, mind, and soul by his Creator and was obligated to use them. They scorned the notion handed down from Puritan forefathers that we are innately evil and incapable of making moral choice. This comfortable way out moved us to laughter in the late 1960s when comedian Flip Wilson's character Geraldine excused her wrongdoing by saying, "The devil made me do it." Now we have seized the major roles in what is either a tragedy or the darkest of comedies, our lines parroting those of Geraldine as we issue disclaimer for annihilation of wildness: "We are only human," we insist. "We cannot be held responsible."

While Emerson and Thoreau recognized our shortcomings, they refused to lose sight of our innate potential to discern right from wrong. Consequently, the plea that we are pawns in the hands of overpowering evil forces is merely an excuse without credibility. They looked at the trumpeting laid down in the Constitution and the Declaration of Independence—those grand implications about the abilities bestowed on us by God to set our own course and to be responsible for the consequences—and threw this promise of greatness back in our faces: we have the capacity to do what is right, they told us, if we are able to move ourselves beyond the influence of what is merely profitable and expedient.

The men from Concord also believed that if God created this planet and all that is on it, then something of the artist, his intent and demeanor, would be reflected in what he made. Thus, the landscape is a sacred trust, a natural scripture wherein spirit waits for those with the patience to discern it. Emily Dickinson understood. From her window in Amherst, Massachusetts, this poet-recluse was privy to all the pages of holy writ necessary to maintain her unflagging faith. While others kept the Sabbath by going to church, Dickinson kept it by staying at home, her tightly penned observations of nature serving as tribute to the force of creation.

In his essay "Self-Reliance," Emerson said, "If a man claims to know and speak of God, and carries you backward to the phraseology of some mouldered nation in another country, in another world, believe him not." Emerson wondered, why search for God in books, in places millennia removed, when he is here now, inextricably fused to the land? We long for the separation of time. Its passage will allow the stories to evolve into myth and magic and substitute for firsthand experience by taking us back to the days of miracles when angels and burning bushes provided instruction. We want easy answers, direct quotations from above, guidelines set in stone and carried down the mountain. Perhaps the mountain would speak as fluently as what is written on the stone if only we would pause to listen and wonder. Instead, we opt for one-liners from the Good Book, favorite verses used to reflexively rebut anything that does not conform to the standards of the narrow litmus test we have deemed to be Truth, for once-a-week absolution accompanied by spiritual inoculation from men of the cloth with a direct pipeline to the designs of the Creator. Most often, we would rather not be asked to think at all. If salvation could be taken as a pill, we would open wide and swallow.

Emerson and Thoreau knew that any of us could find God, that truth was not rationed out on the seventh day in buildings with pews and stained glass where ritual chanting took the place of the transcendent workings of heart and mind. God was readily available, always on call. He could be found in the very place over which we were given dominion. He is still there, I am certain, though we have done what we can to extinguish his presence.

"The cost of a thing," Thoreau noted in *Walden,* "is the amount of life which must be exchanged for it, immediately or in the long run." As salmon fail to return to streams clotted with silt washed from a denuded landscape, as the riparian system is poisoned by pesticide runoff condoned by our representatives in Washington, as wolves become only a haunting memory of a Garden clear-cut and poisoned, our response has been to pull on blinders and bow our necks. We are paying dearly for our sins, but haven't bothered to look closely enough to understand the price. Or perhaps we know what we will see and simply refuse to consider that we have conspired to work a deal, an environmental mortgage, which we will bequeath like a genetic disease to our grandchildren.

In his poem "Miracles," Walt Whitman spoke of the marvels contained in our everyday lives. Whitman didn't wait for images of the Virgin Mary to reveal themselves in garage-sale paintings. He saw the dynamics of creation in the world around him, in the symmetry of the webs of spiders, the homely songs of laborers, the artistry of silent, starry skies. Surrounded by such wonders, Whitman asked, "Who makes much of a miracle? As for me, I know of nothing else but miracles."

Like Whitman, I have found miracles of my own: life sprung from the rich red decay of cull logs, the frenzied yip-and-howl of coyotes celebrating a kill, the sibilance of wind caught in the boughs of evergreens. I am content to worship in my own way, with a stump as my pew, the hymns of chipping sparrows as my song of faith, the tracks of deer as the markings that tell the stories of salvation, the rain as my communion wine, the single word of the owl as my testament.

We would do well to reexamine the birthright we have defined for ourselves in Genesis 1:26. The time has come to offer up some healing of our own to the world we have worked so hard to deface, before wildness becomes nothing but a memory. For when we have finally subdued the planet, broken the pieces on the chain of life and sucked them dry, we will be left only with each other to examine and exploit. The spirit will leave us then. We will be lost and there will be no way home.

Where the
River Runs Silver

UST WEST OF MY HOMETOWN OF CASTLE ROCK, WASHINGTON, Four Corners Grocery sells and rents smelt poles during the winter months. They stand outside, propped against the north end of the building like stiff stalks of spaghetti. The poles come out every year at the news that some fisherman at the mouth of the Columbia River has spotted a few smelt near Buoy Ten. They sometimes remain well after the bulk of the run has passed through, leaving the idea of smelt to linger as advertisement for tourists naive enough to believe that the poles mean fish are actually in the river.

I once fell for a similar marketing strategy while visiting California, where I became a victim of the economics of grunion runs and Orange County folktales. On my brother-in-law's promise of wonders found only in the Golden State, we spent an hour looking for parking at Huntington Beach, staked out a place in the sand, rented a pole, and waited for the water to boil with the arrival of the mysterious grunions. The evening was wonderful, filled with good conversation around a driftwood fire, the ocean doing its best to hush us with surf. Though we stayed well into the night, regularly testing the water with a dip, no grunions made the wild dash to the shoreline to lodge in our net. I decided grunion runs were a fabrication on the same level as snipe hunting. I left my brother-in-law with an invitation to come to the Northwest when the smelt were running, so that he could share in a harvest more tangible than his L.A. fable.

I have faith in smelt, perhaps because they've run through the years of my life like the cyclical blessings of wild blackberries and Canada geese. They are part of the lore of the Northwest, where the abridged remains of forests and rivers hold tight to the mystery and bounty that root us in the land of wintergreen. Each day, the broad-stroked image that has been the American West edges away from reality and closer to the abyss where myth alone can tell the story. But for now, though their numbers are diminished, this portion of the tale comes to life each time the smelt return in schools from the Pacific, fighting their way up the Columbia to spawn in the Cowlitz and Lewis Rivers.

Six to nine inches in length, smelt are cousins of the herring. Members of the family Osmeridae of the order Clupeiformes, they serve as an important link on the food chain as feed for salmon, sturgeon, seals, and sea lions. The most likely time for their arrival is between January and April, though fore-telling precisely when they will come, or even if they will make an appearance during any given year, is nearly as tricky as predicting weather in June. I have a sister-in-law who is much the same. You can try to schedule her, make out an itinerary months in advance, but she refuses to succumb to people's attempts to organize her movements. You've been led to believe she will fly in for Christmas or a summer holiday—she has assured you on the telephone more than once—but experience has made you cautious about wagering the house on such assurances. When she does arrive, sweeping into town like a night heron, there is magic. She is the current missing from the stream of our hearts, and her return to us is not taken lightly.

Smelt runs bring a carnival atmosphere to the ten-mile stretch from Kelso to Castle Rock. People roll in from Oregon, eastern Washington, Puget Sound, British Columbia, nudging their Bounders and Winnebagos through town, lining the riverbanks and congesting traffic along Westside Highway and Pleasant Hill Road. Explaining why they come is not as easy as it might seem. Sure, smelt taste fine, although in the Northwest, where fish are as much a part of the lifestyle as venison and fresh strawberries, their flavor is nothing special. Each year I eat one mess, maybe a dozen smelt, rolled in cornmeal and quick-fried, and that satisfies me until the next run comes through. Smelt dippers are allowed twenty pounds of fish per day, but factor in the cost of gas for the trips down the interstate or across the Cascades, calculate the money spent on food and sundries, and a few pounds of smelt doesn't seem to be much of a bargain.

I suppose an innate sense of greed, the kind that compels squirrels to cache what they cannot use, could suffice as motive, but the allure of the event cannot be explained away by instinct or profit. I've come to believe people are drawn to smelt dipping by some combination of mystery and magic and hope, none of which are particularly accessible anymore. We are like youngsters set to embark on an evening of trick-or-treat, high-schoolers preparing for the prom. It is Christmas and birthdays, the stuff that sets people talking. We can never be sure what is held for us beneath the water, but we can make a wish and hope a gift will be delivered, circumstantial evidence that the land has not forsaken us in the face of our betrayal.

I enjoy dipping smelt at night. When they are running strong, you can shine your light on the water and see the wriggling stream of silver-black shimmering through the beam like a thick muddle of runaway cells under a microscope, a strand of electric satin, reflected and refracted. There is power in their surge against the current, irrepressible energy rippling like a tendon. Along the riverbanks, fires burn like matches struck in the darkness. From each fire, there is holiday-style chatter and a spirit of harvest that binds people like family through an evening.

Occasionally, my daughters accompany me. They don't care for the taste of smelt, but they are drawn by the adventure, the sheer delight of pulling something wild from the river. When I was a boy, the smelt pole we used had a wooden handle an inch and a half in diameter and required Paul Bunyan to operate it effectively. Now we use a pole that was my father-in-law's. It has a twelve-foot telescoping aluminum handle with the equivalent of a basketball net—tighter mesh, sewn shut at the bottom—attached to the end. When my daughters were younger, it took both of them to handle the pole. Now each can manage on her own, and we trade off every few minutes, sharing the celebration as we share each other's company.

Smelt dipping is easily mastered. You work the net in upstream, keeping the rim perpendicular to the water, dragging it low, maybe bouncing it off the bottom as you pull it downstream. The smelt bump against the back of the net like plums dropped into a bag as you struggle to keep the current from rolling it over. You might get nothing, or you might snag six or seven.

I've also seen times when the net couldn't hold all the smelt trying to fight their way in, maybe fifteen pounds in a single dip. In the beam of the flashlight, they were less individuals than an empowered silver force. Regardless of the result, my daughters are not concerned about taking fish home. They simply empty the contents of the net into the river after each dip.

Their grandfather loved fishing more than anything except family—and when the fish were in the river our position at the top of his list seemed tenuous indeed. The son of a Kentucky coal miner, James Carter worked the mines himself before his heart told him that unless he broke the string, his children would end up in the same place, living with the specter of cave-ins and black lung disease. After a stopover in Indiana, he moved west to Riverside, California, searching for the dream that America has always placed out west. He soon realized, however, that California wasn't what he'd hoped. There were too many people, too much pollution, congestion, and crime, so he continued his quest for a place that fit.

He drove up the coast to check for work and find a home, finally settling on southwest Washington. There was room here, a chance to have a dog that didn't have to be relegated to a cage in the backyard, places for kids to run, to stretch their muscles and unhinge their hearts. And, of course, there was the fishing. After he'd landed a job as an electrician with Reynolds Metals Company in Longview, the family followed him north in 1969. I didn't learn their history until the following year, when James Carter's search for place brought me his daughter, the woman who is my wife and the mother of my children.

James didn't drift fish and wasn't particularly interested in buying a boat. For the most part, he was content to plunk with a lure and sinker or do a little casting. I hadn't fished for a long while, but he coaxed me, set me up with a rig, and finally I relented. In spring and summer we fished for harvest trout with spoons at Coal Mine Hole south of town. The place is unrecognizable now, trees and riffles scraped away by the flood that followed the eruption of Mt. St. Helens in 1980, but I can still smell the water, cool and musky, and hear the breeze sweeping through the cottonwoods. In fall, we fished for salmon in the deep hole below the Rock, where a strike from a big chinook could tear the line off your reel no matter how tight the drag. Winter meant steelhead fishing, his favorite. He liked to build a fire in a five-gallon bucket, rig a spin-glow or flat fish, secure his pole in a pole holder, then sit back and watch the river idle by. If the weather was bad, we'd hunker beneath plastic sheeting he'd hung for shelter. And if nothing was going in the Cowlitz, we fished for cats and sunfish and bass at Silver Lake, or made the trek to the jetty at Long Beach to try our luck with perch and sea bass.

Given a choice, you'd think that wrestling thirty-pound chinooks or witnessing the lightning power and muscular aerobatics of steelhead would have most impressed a Kentucky-born Californian learning to be a Northwesterner. But smelt were the marvel that solidified his belief that this was the place he'd been coming home to all his life. In winter months, he'd scan the local paper for information, some sign that they'd entered the Columbia and were headed our way. He bought a pole and a smoker, kept smelt in the refrigerator in the garage and ate them for snacks, almost as though he was pulling a fast one on the forces that twist our lives.

When James died in 1978, his relatives came out from Indiana for the funeral. It was January and the smelt were in the river early that year. When we took the brothers-in-law smelt dipping at Rocky Point north of Kelso, they were like kids on Christmas morning, arguing about whose turn it was to use the pole, chortling over every netful. They ignored my warning that we were close to our limits and risking a fine. Reasonably certain that the game warden would not excuse the excesses of the Happy Hoosiers, I finally had to wrestle the pole away from them and strap them in the car. When we got home, I cleaned smelt for two hours while they sat in the living room and rattled on as though they'd landed world-class marlin. Until that day, their fishing had been relegated to pay ponds; now they had visited a place where a man could stand on the riverbank and dip fish out by the basketful. They were still talking about it when they left for Indiana, as if to convince themselves that what they had seen was more than a yarn.

For a time I wondered at the great struggle of smelt, fighting so hard and traveling so many miles just to find the right place to die. I think I understand it better now, though it is easy to let the dying get in the way. The most important thing is making your way to the destination we call home, where belonging is as seamless as smelt slipping through winter water. Unlike my father-in-law, I have not been forced to seek it out, but I am anchored here as firmly as he was, guyed like a spar tree in a landscape where clear days mean sky blue as the bottom of a pool, where rain paints the hills in greens that stretch the imagination, and where when luck is with us for those few weeks in winter, the river runs silver.

The smelt didn't make it this year in numbers significant enough to be called a run. Biologists have begun to express concern about the future of smelt populations as we suffer though our second consecutive year of radically reduced catches—down nearly 85 percent from record years in the late 1980s and early '90s. No one can be sure if the cause is drought or dams or El Niño, only that a treasure we have taken for granted may soon go the way of old-growth forests and native steelhead.

In the meantime, we will wait for smelt as we wait for the sister-in-law who conforms to no schedule other than her own: with fingers crossed, hoping that next year their inexplicable run for an impulse will bring them home.

About the Author

James LeMonds has lived most of his life in Castle Rock, Washington, a logging town in the shadow of Mt. St. Helens. The son of a log-truck driver, LeMonds has worked on a railroad section crew, in the woods setting chokers, and in a brewery. He holds a master's degree in education from Lewis and Clark College and teaches English at R. A. Long High School in Longview, Washington.

—Emily Minium photo

We encourage you to patronize your local bookstores. Most stores will order any title that they do not stock. You may also order directly from Mountain Press by mail, using the order form provided below, or by calling our toll-free number and using your Visa or Mastercard. We will gladly send you a complete catalog upon request.

Some other Mountain Press Publishing titles of interest:

____Alpine Wildflowers of the Rocky Mountains	$14.00
____Birds of the Pacific Northwest Mountains	$14.00
____Chief Joseph and the Nez Perces	$15.00
____Children of the Fur Trade	$15.00
____Coastal Wildflowers of the Pacific Northwest	$14.00
____Edible and Medicinal Plants of the West	$21.00
____Fire Mountains of the West	$16.00
____Graced by Pines The Ponderosa Pine in the American West	$10.00
____Grinnell's Glacier	$10.00
____Hollows, Peepers, and Highlanders An Appalachian Mountain Ecology	$14.00
____The Lochsa Story Land Ethics in the Bitterroot Mountains	$20.00
____Mountain Plants of the Pacific Northwest	$20.00
____Northwest Exposures A Geologic Story of the Northwest	$24.00
____Northwest Weeds The Ugly and Beautiful Villains of Fields, Gardens, and Roadsides	$14.00
____OWLS Whoo are they?	$12.00
____The Ranch	$14.00
____The Range	$14.00
____Roadside History of California	$18.00
____Roadside History of Idaho	$18.00
____Roadside History of Oregon	$18.00
____Sagebrush Country A Wildflower Sanctuary	$14.00

Please include $3.00 per order to cover shipping and handling.

Send the books marked above. I enclosed $ _____

Name_____

Address _____

City _____ State _____ Zip _____

☐ Payment enclosed (check or money order in U.S. funds)

Bill my: ☐ VISA ☐ MasterCard Expiration Date:_____

Card No _____

Signature_____

Mountain Press Publishing Company
P.O. Box 2399 • Missoula, MT 59806
Order Toll Free 1-800-234-5308
E-mail: mtnpress@montana.com
Have your Visa or MasterCard ready.